Drawing Strength
from the
Right Sources

A Book of Inspiration

By Chris Goppert

WESTBOW
PRESS®
A DIVISION OF THOMAS NELSON
& ZONDERVAN

WestBow Press books may be ordered through booksellers or by contacting:

WestBow Press
A Division of Thomas Nelson & Zondervan
1663 Liberty Drive
Bloomington, IN 47403
www.westbowpress.com
1 (866) 928-1240

Because of the dynamic nature of the Internet, any web addresses or links contained in this book may have changed since publication and may no longer be valid. The views expressed in this work are solely those of the author and do not necessarily reflect the views of the publisher, and the publisher hereby disclaims any responsibility for them.

Any people depicted in stock imagery provided by Thinkstock are models, and such images are being used for illustrative purposes only. Certain stock imagery © Thinkstock.

Cover by Sharon Dahl

ISBN: 978-1-5127-9308-6 (sc)
ISBN: 978-1-5127-9307-9 (hc)
ISBN: 978-1-5127-9309-3 (e)

Library of Congress Control Number: 2017910432

Print information available on the last page.

WestBow Press rev. date: 03/08/2019

The Suffering We Endure Today[1]

Endure hardship with us as a good soldier of Christ Jesus.
—2 Tim. 2:3 (NIV)

In just a few words, the apostle Paul reveals to Timothy that suffering is a corporate reality, in that we do not suffer in isolation, but as a members of the royal band of faithful warriors.

Charles Colson expands on this observation with incisive clarity and practical application, when he notes that the suffering we endure today, becomes our participation in establishing Christ's victory.
—Charles Colson

Ill fortune never crushed that man, whom good fortune deceived not![2]
—Ben Jonson (1573)

It has been intimated that this somewhat novel book (being not a novel in the traditional sense) may in time become an ideal bathroom book for weary souls. The author, who apologizes profusely for any grammatical or formatting gremlins that may still be lurking in the woodwork of said publication, is rather inclined to concur.

More to the point, however, is that the central intent of this publication is not to answer the perennially big *why* question of suffering. Rather, it is designed to direct the reader toward knowing more about the larger and more important *who* and *how* aspects of this important topic.

By focusing on the *who* aspect, relative to the place for suffering in life, one is then led to appreciate that God is and will remain unquestionably good and trustworthy, and that His gracious will (Eph. 1:5–11) allows for suffering and hardship in accordance with the integrity of His heart and in the outworking of His inscrutable, but all-wise purposes for time and eternity.

Having properly engaged the indispensable *who* aspect of the matter, we can more easily segue into the *how* factor, or the ability of processing and coming to terms with our trials and afflictions. Once we settle in our minds that God is good and faithful, we will find the necessary strength of heart to persevere in the hard times, and the ability to maintain a high view of God's integrity of heart when we do not hear His voice in the *storm*.

Where possible, the author has attempted to retain the current American spelling of all words, unless a direct quote or use of the KJV version of the Bible required the use of the Queen's English.

I tell you the truth, you will weep and mourn while the world rejoices.
You will grieve, but your grief will turn to joy.
—John 16:20 (NIV)

I remember my affliction and my wandering, the bitterness and the gall. I well remember them, and my soul is downcast within me. Yet, this I call to mind and therefore I have hope: Because of the Lord's great love we are not consumed, for His compassions never fail.
—Lamentations 3:19–22 (NIV)

C.S. Lewis expresses well the importance of having a correct mindset to offset the potentially debilitating effects of bitterness and despair amidst one's afflictions. He wrote,

At first I am overwhelmed …
then I try to bring myself into the frame of mind I should be
in at all times … I become a creature consciously dependent
upon God, drawing its strength from the right sources.[3]

It's Not Spiritual[4]

When you're cold and wet,
It's not spiritual to say that you're
warm and dry.

—Wilf Strom

To our courageous friends who, through unwavering
faith, have silenced the lies of the slanderer and
exhibited uncommon grace under
incredible pressure.

May your precious faith, dear friends, continue to exemplify an
unwavering heartfelt response to His unfailing faithfulness!

The more imminent the danger; the more eminent the deliverance!
—Source Unknown

Contents

You Will

> For the Lord of hosts will have a day of
> Reckoning against everyone who is proud
> And lofty, and against everyone who is lifted up
> That he may be abased.
>
> —Isa. 2:12 (NASB)

Wayne Grudem captures beautifully the essence of
Isaiah's anticipation of that wondrous day when righteous
judgment will be on display for all to behold.

The fact that there will be a final judgment assures us that ultimately
God's universe is fair, for God is in control.[5]

> Though you have made me see
> Troubles, many and bitter,
> *You will* restore my life again;
> From the depths of the earth
> *You will* again bring me up.
> *You will* increase my honor
> And comfort me once again.
>
> —Psalm 71:20–21 (NIV)

A Bruised Reed He Will Not Break

A bruised reed he will not break,

And a smoldering wick he will not snuff out. In faithfulness, he
will bring forth justice; He will not falter or be discouraged
Until he establishes justice on earth.

In his law the islands will put their hope.

—Isaiah 42:3–4 (NIV)

Foreword

Like an old country doctor dispensing medicine—"Take one of these each day for the next thirty-one days"—Chris Goppert offers his prescription for those suffering from the struggles of life. But the truth he is dispensing comes directly from the Bible—healing and comforting words from the Great Physician.

At a time when scores of devotional guides crowd bookstore shelves, *Drawing Strength from the Right Sources* stands apart from the rest. It is a one-month devotional guide that is easy to read, insightful, biblically accurate, and intensely relevant.

Chris Goppert's skillful handling of God's Word helps the reader discover the relevance of passages that put our daily struggles into their eternal perspective. And each lesson ends with a burst of practical insights that comes out of Goppert's own personal experience.

My advice? Buy two copies of the book. Read one yourself and give the second copy to a friend. Then watch God work in both your lives as He teaches you to draw your strength from the right sources!

—Dr. Charles H. Dyer, professor-at-large of Bible;
radio host of *The Land and the Book*

Therefore, since the children share in flesh and blood, He Himself
Likewise also partook of the same, that through death, He might
Render powerless him who had the power of death, that is, the devil.
—Heb. 2:14 (NASB)

In just a few poignant words, Yancey summarizes the truth of the
above passage from Hebrews 2, when he notes, that He (Christ)
has dignified for all time those who suffer, by sharing their pain.[6]
—Philip Yancey

Powerful Truths from Psalm 23[7]

Suffering with stage four breast/bone cancer is helping me rediscover powerful and comforting truths from Psalm 23:

> "He prepares a table before me in the presence of my enemies."

When my all loving Father chooses not to remove my enemies of pain, fear and suffering, He always promises His tangible presence with deep, satisfying fellowship as we dine—just the two of us, seated closely together—in the midst of these standing foes. —Deborah Colones

Acknowledgments

With sincerest appreciation to:

Doug, who encouraged me to write about issues associated with various trials of faith.

Mary and Naomi, who served as the catalysts of inspiration for this project.

Sharon, for the compellingly creative front cover.

Terry and Gail, for their wonderful encouragement and loving affirmation that carried us through the moments of uncertainty about this project.

The good folk at Link-Care, for their compassionate and professional ministry of restoration and counsel.

C. S. Lewis, whose exhortation for a believer to be a creature who *draws its strength from the right sources* inspired me to adapt that concept for the title of this publication.

Kim and Sonja, who worked assiduously in the background vetting the grammatical gremlins, confirming bibliographic data, and locating websites of publishers whose material is cited in this publication.

The tireless efforts of proof readers and copy editors, who exhibited generous displays of patience, love, professional insights, faithful editing, and invaluable comments. Special words of appreciation also go to so many friends who vetted the material for me and provided feedback and affirmation, including Norm, Onesimus, Alistair, Josh, Eugene, Ron, Charlie, Samantha, Ross, Phil, Brian, Sandra, Kayla, and Roy. Well done, good friends.

Steve, for his helpful insights and assistance that enabled us to make the necessary transition from a spiral-bound seminar booklet to a professionally bound book.

The editorial staff at WestBow Press for their indispensable critiques.

Ken, for providing the original concept of *Parking Our Minds in the Right Place*.

Joyce, my gracious wife, who kindly allowed me to descend the stairs to the basement office more times than I could possibly count, so that I could give myself to the foundational stages of this publication (Eccl. 3:1–8). You're the best!

Our most gracious savior and Lord Jesus, to whom belongs all honor and praise for His unfailing love, tender mercies, and restorative touch.

Introduction

In his peerless book the *Dust Diaries*, Owen Sheers relates the stirring account of Captain Richard Meinertzhagen's experience of encountering severely wounded soldiers. As he walked toward the German Schutztruppe headquarters to negotiate a British surrender and withdrawal from East Africa, Meinertzhagen heard British wounded soldiers calling out to him for help in their various native languages. "In their distress, though, they all sounded the same; pain, as he had learnt years ago, was a language that crossed all borders."[8]

Inasmuch as incidences of catastrophic tragedies, personal suffering, and pain are surfacing in waves of unprecedented universal proportions—yes, touching us with increased frequency via the media and in the lives of friends and family—people in quiet desperation (and not so, at times) are longing for insights and assurances that will not only help them to find the strength of heart to go on, but to make sense of some of the complexities surrounding suffering, and hopefully fit it altogether into a greater, more meaningful picture.

Though many people in our day have been spared from the painful nightmares associated with a debilitating disease, the Holocaust, the loss of a loved one on 9/11, the Boston Marathon attack, the Columbine massacre, famine, statelessness brought about by state-sponsored emigration, loss of a home from a hurricane or fire, and scars inflicted during apartheid or by rape, the fact remains that countless people, universally, are suffering in some way and are hoping to work through their own very real and yet, private nightmares, (financial reversal, divorce or the prospect of dying) without losing faith or the heart to carry on, and in turn, avoid becoming embittered by such experiences.

To this end, *Drawing Strength from the Right Sources* provides insightful commentary on various issues relating to suffering and hardship. From a sound theological base, this book affirms that God remains unquestionably good, even though He may ordain, within the context of

His perfect will, that His followers will experience refining grace whilst suffering within the counsel of His good will.

Therefore, without attempting to supply final or definitive answers to the many nagging questions relating to why God may allow suffering, *Drawing Strength from the Right Sources* sets out rather to bring to the reader's heart assurances regarding what we may know to be true about God in our afflictions. Briefly then, the overarching intent of this work is to encourage the afflicted friend to continually trust in the Lord's integrity of heart, so that he does not cave in to bewilderment associated with God's seeming silence and mysterious ways that permit hardships to befall us.

Furthermore, this publication seeks to affirm that potential disillusionment with God, as expressed by Screwtape's "Inarticulate resentment with which we teach them to respond,"[9] is not our only option when we find ourselves mystified by God's inscrutable ways. Rather, on a practical note, this book seeks to provide a means for enabling disheartened friends to derive spiritual strength from the right sources (see: 1 Sam. 23:16—David found his strength in the Lord), by revisiting what we know to be true about God's integrity of heart.

> When we are in a panic, it's useful to gain the support of trusted friends.
> Friendship enables us to take our fears out from the labyrinth that is our mind, with all of its shadows and dark corners;
> Enriched by the insights of fellow travelers, we are able to see our challenges more clearly.
> Elijah, turned his back on this, and allowed fear to do what fear so often does: shunt him into isolation.[10]
> —Jeff Lucas

In this regard, Spurgeon said, "Let your heart be glad, O believer, but take care that your gladness has its spring in the Lord."[11] When his life was threatened, King David "encouraged himself *in the Lord his God*"

(1 Sam. 30:6 KJV)! Consistent with Spurgeon's words, a son of Korah wrote, "All my springs *are in thee*" (Ps. 87:7 KJV).

The series of devotional studies found in part II are based in part on teaching originally given by the author in various pastoral care settings in a third-world country overwhelmed by severe suffering and grief. The reader is encouraged to view this book then as a genuinely humble yet sincere attempt on the author's part to relay some truths the Lord has been pleased to use to sustain many of the Lord's good people (the writer, himself, notwithstanding) through various heavy seasons of trials of faith.

Having attempted in some small measure to address the subject of suffering in its varying and manifold contexts, I hasten to add that I am not claiming to be an authority on this vastly complex subject. Nor am I saying I have learned the totality of any one spiritual truth highlighted in these pages. Instead, I am attempting to say that the principles I write about point rather to the utter faithfulness of the Lord to sustain one in and through various trials to our faith.

The themes and truths discussed in this work have ministered grace to my soul and poignantly echo the truth of the words of a young believer who declared, "I always knew the Christian faith was true, but I never realized it was this true!"

Having once experienced suffering, we find a discernible thread common to the Christian experience, where a dominant pressure point or protracted burden of heart exposes our inadequacies and utter sense of helplessness. At this point, God will begin to wean us, in a profound way, from self-reliance, human wisdom, and cleverly-devised coping techniques, or as Watchman Nee would say, "being fundamentally weakened at our natural point of power."[12] The result will be a renewed discovery of the wonders of His unfailing mercies and the sufficiency of His matchless grace (2 Cor. 1:8–10).

The pressure points or burdens may take the form of a personal thorn in the flesh, a family relational issue, or a health, ministerial, financial, or national crisis. However, irrespective of the nature of the pressure point, it will not only be used by the Lord to bring us to the end of our self-reliance, but it will lead us to do a number of other significant things.

First and foremost, will be the revisiting (not rethinking) of what we know to be true about the Lord. Martin Luther said to the Dutch scholar Erasmus, "Your thoughts of God are too human,"[13] which rightly suggests that an inadequate knowledge of God leads to an inadequate trust of God.

(cont'd...)

In My Distress, I Called to the Lord

From inside the fish Jonah prayed to the Lord his God. He
said: *"In my distress, I called to the Lord*, and he answered
me. From the depths of the grave I called for
help, and you listened to my cry.
"You hurled me into the deep, into the very heart of the seas, and the
currents swirled about me; all your waves and breakers swept over me.
"I said, 'I have been banished from your sight; yet
I will look again toward your holy temple.'
"The engulfing waters threatened me, the deep surrounded
me; seaweed was wrapped around my head.
"To the roots of the mountains I sank down; the
earth beneath barred me in forever.
"But you brought my life up from the pit, O Lord my God.
"When my life was ebbing away, I remembered you, Lord,
and my prayer rose to you, to your holy temple.
"Those who cling to worthless idols forfeit
the grace that could be theirs.
"But I, with a song of thanksgiving, will sacrifice to you.
"What I have vowed I will make good.
"Salvation comes from the Lord."

—Jonah 2:1–9 (NIV)

As we seek to make better sense of what is happening to us during a trial or burden of heart, we come to appreciate more clearly the multiple facets of God's person, His attributes and ways, and thus His supreme trustworthiness.

Secondly, the pressure point will lead us to a deeper understanding of the Lord's pastoral heart for His people's spiritual welfare. Having entered the realm of the fellowship of His sufferings (from our own personal experience with pain), we will learn what actually burdens and "breaks" the heart of God (Phil. 3:10c; 1 Pet. 4:13).

Third, convinced of the Lord's gentle pastoral care for our hearts, spiritual burdens will invariably instill within us a thirst to find meaningful, substantial answers to our heart cry (*cri de coeur*) from His good hand. Such a sincere desire, that is open to God, will in turn move us to draw vital spiritual strength from the right sources (Acts 20:32) and not from trite, inane bumper-sticker theology or superficial, warm-fuzzy platitudes dispensed at the local pub or around the office coffee urn.

Understandably, if there are right sources for appropriating grace, then it may be correctly assumed there are wrong sources. Right sources, such as the eternal truth of God's Word, which undergirds and refreshes the soul in seasons of heaviness (Ps. 119:92), and the testimony of tried and approved saints can easily be identified by their ability to enable one to discover enduring and effectual spiritual strength (inspiration, mercy, hope, faith, truth, and endurance). Conversely, wrong sources provide nothing of enduring hope or encouragement in grace, nor persevering trust in the integrity of Christ's heart for our good and His glory.

As much as I would dearly love to be able to provide my readers with specific answers as to why there is suffering in this life, I cannot so presume, nor dare.

Suffice it to say then, when there are no answers, there are the assurances of God's faithfulness, goodness, and integrity of heart. If this publication accomplishes nothing else other than encouraging the reader to continue to worship God, to esteem Him worthy of further trust, and to not accept trite answers, which may preclude us from finding Him, then it will have been worth the endeavor.

Finally, may I take a moment to encourage all who are facing what seem to be endless trials and hardships, to continue to persevere in hope, with the incredible grace that only Jesus, the Son of God, can impart to weary hearts and minds. My prayer is that by totally embracing Jesus, you may find renewed faith and, in the process, discover Him to be the sympathetic Man of Sorrows who is fully acquainted with our grief.

Having then embraced Jesus as the true Man of Sorrows, may you the reader, find renewed courage and the heart to endure by leaning hard on His everlasting arms (Deut. 33:27). So, with renewed zeal, may you joyfully and continually draw your daily, spiritual strength from the right sources provided by God in Christ through His most excellent Word.

Sincerely, the author!

In Our Shattered Times[14]

In our shattered times, anguish relents not at mere idle words
spoken in vain, But rather from the silent eloquence
Bestowed by those rare souls who share our pain.
—Evans (cited by Yancey)

And our hope for you is firm, because we know that just as you
share in our sufferings, so also you share in our comfort.
—2 Cor. 1:7 (NIV)

No, that trauma you faced was not easy.
And God wept that it hurt you so;
But it was allowed to shape your heart, so
that into His likeness you'd grow.[15]
—Russell Kelfer

But we all, with unveiled face, beholding as in a mirror the glory of
The Lord, are being transformed into the same image from glory to
Glory, just as from the Lord, the Spirit.
—2 Cor. 3:18 (NASB)

Blessed Be Your Name[16]
by Beth and Matt Redman

Blessed be your name
When the sun's shining down on me
When the world's all as it should be
Blessed be your name

Blessed be your name
On the road marked with suffering
Though there's pain in the offering
Blessed be your name

Every blessing you pour out, I turn back to praise
When the darkness closes in, Lord
Still I will say …

Blessed be the name of the Lord
Blessed be your name
Blessed be the name of the Lord
Blessed be your glorious name

You give and take away
You give and take away
My heart will choose to say
Lord, Blessed be your name.

He stretches us farther, so that we will look at Him harder.[17]
—Dr. Ross McCordic

When I Am in Distress

Do not hide your face from me
When I am in distress.
Turn your ear to me; when I call,
Answer me quickly.
—Psalm 102:2 (NIV)

Part I

You are my refuge in the day of disaster.
—Jeremiah 17:17 (ESV)

It Was for My Benefit That I Suffered

A writing of Hezekiah king of Judah after his illness and recovery:

"I cried like a swift or thrush, I moaned like a mourning dove. My eyes grew weak as I looked to the heavens. 'I am troubled; O Lord, come to my aid!'

"But what can I say? He has spoken to me, and he himself has done this. I will walk humbly all my years because of this anguish of my soul.

"Lord, by such things men live; and my spirit finds life in them too. You restored me to health and let me live.

"*Surely it was for my benefit that I suffered such anguish.* In your love, you kept me from the pit of destruction; you have put all my sins behind your back.

"For the grave cannot praise you, death cannot sing your praise; those who go down to the pit cannot hope for your faithfulness.

"The living, the living—they praise you, as I am doing today; fathers tell their children about your faithfulness.

"The Lord will save me, and we will sing with stringed instruments all the days of our lives in the temple of the Lord."

—Isaiah 38:9; 14–20 (NIV)

Knowing Heart-Rest When Bewildered by God's Inscrutable Ways

Finding Our Way out from the Dark Lands of Disillusionment

My flesh and my heart may fail, but God is the strength of my heart.
—Psalm 73:26 (NIV)

The book of Ecclesiastes encourages us to rejoice in the good years and to also remember the days of darkness, for they will be many.[18]

For a moment, if the reader will indulge me, I want to reflect on a significant segment of time in our life, characterized by more than its *fair* share of distress and grief, with a view to considering lessons learned regarding the importance of trusting the essential goodness of God, when all I could see about me was the exceeding wickedness of humanity, or so it seemed. During that time, I often felt like the Old Testament writer, who, when stricken with anguish of heart and fear, longed to flee to a desert place to find solitude and refuge for his beleaguered soul.[19]

Have you ever wrestled deeply with the mysterious ways of Providence or questioned why God did not respond to an urgent, heartfelt prayer sooner? Be encouraged, you are not alone. There was a point in my life when I had become thoroughly dismayed by what appeared to be, at the time, the Lord's undisclosed reasons for not intervening in the nightmarish conditions that overwhelmed the beautiful country we had called home for thirty years. Like a blinding, clinging fog, "pain, which cannot forget," as Aeschylus wrote, fell "drop by drop upon the heart,"[20] causing me to stagger about in the dark lands of disillusionment. Essentially, I had allowed myself to become disheartened and dismayed by what was without question our country's darkest hour. But then, slowly, step by step, I came to realize that I could not continue living under the self-imposed pall of this clinging despair and excessive grief that had enveloped my emotions, without reaping the consequence of a debilitating disillusionment with and a distorted view of the essential goodness of God.

Beginning a journey out of the dark lands of one's disillusionment with God's mysterious ways is not necessarily an onerous process or an exercise in futility, but neither is it achieved overnight. Thankfully, the Lord graciously nurtures one in and through this vital healing process. In my particular circumstance, He showed me that I had been needlessly weakening my own emotional and spiritual fortitude by consciously focusing on what I had perceived to be His seeming reluctance to stop the suffering of innumerable people. In fact, what I needed to do was to adopt an entirely different focus, by actively celebrating God's integrity of heart and choosing to concentrate rather on the majesty and wisdom of His providential ways, irrespective of how inscrutable they may have appeared at the time. If you will, God himself needed to become "my dread" (Isa. 8:12–13), instead of allowing what I feared to become an object of paralyzing dismay.

Yet the Lord Rescued Me

You, however, know all about my teaching, my way of life, my purpose, faith, patience, love, endurance, persecutions, sufferings—what kinds of things happened to me in Antioch, Iconium and Lystra, the persecutions I endured. *Yet the Lord rescued me from all of them.*

In fact, everyone who wants to live a godly life in Christ Jesus will be persecuted, while evil men and impostors will go from bad to worse, deceiving and being deceived.

—2 Timothy 3:10–13 (NIV)

This realization opened my eyes to refocus my mental energies on the vital lessons I had once learned to be true in the past about God's integrity of heart.

In retrospect, I am incredibly grateful to the Lord for bringing me out from what can only be described as an extreme and intolerably suffocating blanket of sadness (Ps. 13:2, "[I] have sorrow in my heart every day"), to a place of genuine heart-rest typified by "the garment of praise, instead of a spirit of despair" (Isa. 61:3 NIV).

Certainly, what has become clearer with time is the realization that until God chooses to intervene in our personal nightmares, we can nevertheless find in the interim a settled heart-rest based on the assurance that the Lord remains faithful to His own.

Furthermore, and without any doubt, God will most assuredly and graciously bring about in His perfect time any and all necessary resolution, justice, and relief from suffering, tyranny, and brutality for all who languish under oppressive regimes or in painful circumstances. John Calvin once encouraged suffering believers with these words of grace, "Wherefore, my brethren, when the tyrants exhaust all their fury, learn to turn your eyes to contemplate the succor which God affords his followers; and seeing that they are not forsaken by him, take new comfort and cease not to war against the temptations of your flesh, till you have attained the full conviction that we are happy in belonging to Christ whether it be to die or to live."[21]

With the above assurances in mind, any number of pastors and Bible teachers over the years have encouraged those who question God's love and whether they can continue to trust God or not, with these helpful insights:

> It is at such times when we need to step back and remember that we do not live under the control of chaos or happenstance, but ever under the gracious, loving oversight of our merciful Heavenly Father.[22]

When confronted with injustice in His own life (1 Pet. 2:21-23), the Lord Jesus showed us by example the importance of drawing spiritual strength from the right sources and that one's abiding trust in God's control over even the harshest injustices of life can be traced directly to the assurance of God's faithfulness to uphold those who trust him.

John Piper observes, "He (Jesus) did not need to avenge Himself for all the indignities He suffered, because He entrusted His cause to God. He left vengeance in God's hands..."[23]

Will not the judge of all the earth do right?
—Genesis 18:25 (NIV)

Growing Better, Not Worse[24]

I have seen great beauty of spirit in some who were great sufferers. I have seen men, for the most part, grow better not worse with advancing years, and I have seen the last illness produce treasures of fortitude and meekness from most unpromising subjects ...

—C. S. Lewis

A crown of beauty instead of ashes.

—Isa. 61:3

Perhaps it may prove helpful at this point to clarify a few thoughts. First, God never says to His children, who do not understand His ways, that they cannot ask Him questions. Second, neither do we ever need to recoil like a frightened child from God's awesome, sovereign presence when seeking refuge from our pain, perplexity, and heaviness of heart; in fact, He welcomes us (with all of our frustrations and fears)! Notice these wonderfully familiar yet refreshing words from Jesus, who said, "Come to me, all you who are weary and burdened, and I will give you rest" (Matt. 11:28 NIV).

In my own struggle with an increasingly impatient pleading attitude (yes, even demanding at times) that the Lord would bring a swift end to the sadness, a cessation of the rampant lawlessness, and a halt to the selective disregard for human rights that had seized our fair land, He urged me to cast my cares on Him (Ps. 55:22), so as to find rest in the immensity of His wise and gracious sovereign ways.

In his book *The Trivialization of God,* Donald McCullough provides this wise insight:

> When we come to know our 'not-knowing', when we understand the depths of our ignorance...we may indeed find both a freedom from having to know it all and a humble civility to check our strutting tongues.[25]

In essence then, I realized that God was gently prompting me to take heart by waiting on and trusting in the outworking of His overall sovereign designs, irrespective of how long that might be. Such a confident restfulness of heart was known by those who composed the sixteenth-century Heidelberg Catechism:

> I believe in God the Father Almighty, Maker of heaven and earth who out of nothing created heaven and earth ...
>
> I trust in Him so completely that I have no doubt that He will provide me with all things necessary for body

and soul. Moreover, whatever evil He sends upon me in this troubled life He will turn to my good, for He is able to do it, being almighty God and He is determined to do it, being a faithful father.[26]

When I eventually began to trust in and celebrate the integrity of God's heart, I became increasingly refreshed and uplifted in spirit. What a difference it made to learn to rest in the assurance of His absolute control in all of life's circumstances and to come to know and enjoy His perfect peace in my heart; yes, the gracious gift of "heart-rest."

By "heart-rest" I am referring to a frame of mind where a resolute trust springs up from a settled-ness of spirit and where a welcome dispelling of anxiety about the outcome of life's mysteries prevails, even if the riddles continue to defy explanation. In this regard, I appreciate what John Eldredge has written: "The more comfortable we are with mystery in our journey, the more rest we will know along the way."[27]

By Faith He Persevered

By faith Moses, when he had grown up, refused to be known as the son of Pharaoh's daughter.

He chose to be mistreated along with the people of God rather than to enjoy the pleasures of sin for a short time.

He regarded disgrace for the sake of Christ as of greater value than the treasures of Egypt, because he was looking ahead to his reward.

By faith he left Egypt, not fearing the king's anger; *he persevered* because he saw him who is invisible.

—Hebrews 11:24–27 (NIV)

When the way God has marked out for us appears strangely inscrutable (seemingly, to defy any reason), and it remains beyond our ability to comprehend its purpose, it doesn't necessarily mean that the reason will not be made apparent, or that disillusionment or bewilderment with God is our only possible response.

In fact, not having all the answers, all the time, can actually bring relief, clarity, and security in that we are then constrained by faith to cast ourselves on the mercy of God, who is infinitely wiser than we are, and in whose light, we may have insight and hope. Note the following verse: "In thy light, we shall see light" (Ps. 36:9—KJV).

Again, the Lord Jesus said, "I am come as light into the world, so that everyone who believes in me will not remain in darkness" (Jn. 12:46—NASB). In that regard, it may be well for me to tie off a dangling thread that is hanging loose in this conversation. Please understand that I'm not suggesting in any way that if God chooses not to explain his intent of heart behind our momentary afflictions, that we can never know anything else about the Lord's ways or purposes during this life.

In fact, we see in John 15:15 ("all things that I have heard from my Father *I have made known to you*"—KJV*)* and 1 Corinthians 2:10–14 ("but God has revealed it to us through the Spirit"—NIV) that it is possible to have insight into some, if not many of God's ways. Again, Psalm 103:7 (NIV), helps to dispel any doubts in this regard: "He made known His ways to Moses, His deeds to the people of Israel." For further study, the reader will find Genesis 18:17 to be very helpful in this regard, ("Shall I hide from Abraham what I am about to do?" —NASB). The reader may also wish to read Genesis 25:22-23 - Note the "why" question.

Understandably then, when one cannot fathom the depths of God's inscrutable ways, questions are generally not too far off, even when one fully believes in the essential goodness and integrity of God's heart and ways. Note in Jeremiah 12:1 how the prophet affirms his trust in God's righteousness and then poses a familiar question in verse 2, namely: "why does the way of the wicked prosper?"

So, am I suggesting that we should not be asking serious questions or thinking deeply in our attempt to discover whatever insights we can for maintaining spiritual equilibrium and focus? Not at all! Conversely, and most importantly, what I would contend is that we must do all that we can to maintain a firm conviction of heart regarding the essential goodness of God at all times and then consciously trust Him to provide those clarifying rays of comprehension relating to His good purposes in His time and way.

In this regard, John Maxwell comments:

> God doesn't mind questions. It is doubt that He hates. Leaders must never be afraid to ask hard questions of God, but neither must they demand that He answer. And no matter how dark our circumstances may grow, we must resist the temptation to doubt God's holy nature.[28]

Beyond This Vale of Tears[29]
by James Montgomery

Where shall rest be found; Rest for the weary soul?
It were-vain the ocean-depths to sound
Or pierce to either pole.
The world can never give
The bliss for which we sigh
It is not the whole of life to live
Nor all of death to die.
Beyond this vale of tears
There is a life above
Unmeasured by the flight of years
And all that life is love.
There is a death whose pang
Outlasts the fleeting breath.
What eternal horrors hang
Around the second death.
Lord God of truth and grace
Teach us that death to shun
Lest we be banished from thy face
And evermore undone.
Here would we end our quest.
Alone are found in thee
The life of perfect love—the rest
Of immortality.

So there remains a Sabbath rest for the people of God.

> For the one who has entered His rest has himself also
> Rested from his works, as God did from His.
> Therefore, let us be diligent to enter that rest, so that
> No one will fall…
>
> —Heb. 4:9-11 (NASB)

How insightful then to observe in Luke 13 how the Lord Jesus not only welcomes interaction on life's tough questions and hard issues but that He Himself takes the initiative to ask pointed questions in this regard. By virtue of entering into this dialogue, one can appreciate that He wants to draw one out to face the issue squarely and thus bring clarity to the nagging question: is suffering directly related to personal or collective sin?

Consider Jesus's response in the following passage:

> There were some present … who told Jesus about the
> Galileans, whose blood Pilate had mixed with their
> sacrifices. Jesus answered, "Do you think these Galileans
> were worse sinners than all the other Galileans because
> they suffered this way? I tell you, no! But unless you
> repent, you too will all perish (Lk. 13:1-3 NIV).

Thankfully, the Lord responds to the question, but then quickly moves the focus of attention to the more important matter of ensuring that one's personal faith in God is based on a change of attitude and action (repentance).

The upshot then is that our questions are very acceptable, but doubts are out! Again, how helpful it is to realize that if God chooses not to explain why He allows bewildering or painful situations to arise in our lives, it does not mean that He does not care for us or those about us (see how Jesus replied to the above question, thus revealing sensitivity to and awareness of the bewilderment that had surfaced in the enquirer's minds about a legitimate concern).

Furthermore, neither does personal suffering indicate that we have been rejected or abandoned by God. In fact, we will do ourselves an immeasurably great service by accepting by faith the reality that there are times when the Lord reserves the right not to give us immediately satisfying answers to our huge questions (as in the experience of Job), so that we are thereby constrained to fix our attention on the wonder of God's exalted majesty, His overarching, providential purposes and integrity of heart.

This welcome inclination of heart will ensure that we keep leaning hard upon His everlasting arms for grace to persevere in hope, adopting, if you will, a desiring-forward disposition of heart or attitude as we anticipate clarity and resolution, which hopefully will lead to a blessed sense of closure and meaning.

When we can be okay with such an arrangement, we will see that our faith in the Lord will continue to inform and assure our hearts that God will remain ever trustworthy (good at any time—see page 75) and that our hope in Him has not been misplaced, nor will it ever be betrayed.

Even in the Darkness, Light Dawns!

Praise the Lord.
Blessed is the man who fears the Lord,
Who finds great delight in his commands.
His children will be mighty in the land;
The generation of the upright will be blessed.
Wealth and riches are in his house,
And his righteousness endures forever.
Even in darkness light dawns for the upright,
For the gracious and compassionate and
righteous man.
Good will come to him who is generous and lends freely,
Who conducts his affairs with justice.
Surely, he will never be shaken;
A righteous man will be remembered forever.
He will have no fear of bad news;
His heart is steadfast, trusting in the Lord.
His heart is secure. He will have no fear;
In the end, he will look in triumph on his foes.

—Psalm 112:1–8 (NIV)

Over time, I have begun to see that when we can be truly content with not having to figure out completely the mysterious, sovereign purposes of God in their entirety (during the course of our brief lives), and choose rather to make a conscious decision to allow the sovereign Lord to be our refuge (just letting him be God to us and for us), then we will begin to find a stability of heart and mind unlike anything we have ever known. Little wonder then that Isaiah 26:3 (KJV) reads, "thou wilt keep him in perfect peace, whose mind is stayed on thee."

Should we ever be tempted (don't be surprised) to become disillusioned with the bewildering events of our lives, those curious twists that defy credible explanation or where the absurd, according to Donavan Campbell, becomes the baseline, it is good to know that we can still find clarity for a long-term focus and strength in God to fortify our flagging spirits through the faithful counsel of His most excellent Word.

The psalmist wrote, "Unless thy law had been my delights, I should then have perished in mine affliction." (Ps. 119:92 KJV). Thank the Lord for such an incredible confidence and example for us to emulate.

William James put it this way:

> There is a state of mind known to religious people, but to no others, in which the will to assert ourselves and to hold our own has been displaced by a willingness to close our mouths and be as nothing in the floods and waterspouts of God … the time for tension in our soul is over and that of happy relaxation, of calm deep-breathing, of an eternal present with no discordant future to be anxious about has arrived.[30]

In reading through the faith-building experiences of various people in church history and scripture, I find it immensely encouraging to discover that there are not just a few examples of individuals who did not need to *rethink* their view of God when they hit the proverbial wall.

By way of interest, in part IV, one will find testimonies of men and women of faith, just like you and me, who have found God to be immensely faithful and real (yes, in what appeared at the time to be one of the most difficult challenges to their faith walk with Jesus—for whom *light dawned amidst darkness*).

Instead, these faithful saints were strengthened in heart when they allowed their faith to be expanded and renewed by choosing to *revisit* the truths they held dear about God.

> Unless thy law had been my delights, I should
> then have perished in mine affliction.
> —Ps. 119:92 (KJV)

The Unanswered Questions[31]

How pertinent is Augustine's observation with respect to our contemplations regarding why so many questions about life remain un—answered:

> It is better ... to find *You* and leave the questions
> unanswered than to find the answer, without finding *You*.
> —Augustine of Hippo

> Therefore, I have declared that which I did not understand,
> Things too wonderful for me, which I did not know.
> I have heard of You by the hearing of the ear;
> But now my eye sees You;
> Therefore, I retract,
> And I repent in dust and ashes.
> —Job 42:3; 5-6 (NASB)

Such faith-expanding experiences with God not only bring welcome, renewed heart-rest for those who trust Him, but they also affirm what Charles Swindoll once wrote: "Hold on ... do not attempt to re-think God just because hard times come ... hold on tight, because He is doing something great, as He has in the past."[32]

Martin Luther so beautifully captured the essence of Swindoll's exhortation. In one of Luther's darkest hours, he said to his comrades:

> Come, let us sing Psalm 46 and let them do their worst. We sing this Psalm, because God is with us and powerfully and miraculously preserves and defends His church and His word against all fanatical spirits, against the gates of hell, against the implacable hatred of the devil, and against all the assaults of the world.[33]

Clearly, Martin Luther had found in God's Word the right source for offsetting the debilitating effects of doubt and despair's suffocating fog.

Daniel, chapter 3, provides a classic example of how resolute confidence in God is directly linked to our affirming what we know to be true about Him. Several of the Hebrew young men, who had been exiled to Babylon, were threatened with the possibility of losing their lives for not bowing under duress before the king's golden image. When the king heard that the young men would not bow before his image, he exclaimed, "...if you do not worship it, you will be thrown immediately into a blazing furnace. Then what god will be able to rescue you from my hand?" (Dan. 3:15 NIV).

The three young men replied with resolute conviction: "If we are thrown into the blazing furnace, the God whom we serve is able to save us from it, and He will rescue us from your hand, O king" (Dan. 3:17 NIV).

The belief in God's awesome holy person and power, which was formed early in their lives, became the means for establishing their commitment to persevere in faithful obedience in the face of extreme pressure to compromise their faith—yes, even at the point of possibly losing their very lives.

The depth of their implicit trust in God was vindicated through this trial, as God himself, through the manifest presence of His Son, was there in the midst of the ordeal to protect and preserve them from all harm (Dan. 3:25).

Of further significance is the clear message that the Hebrew youths did not have a "bad-day, good-day theology" to see them through life's harsh realities.

A Refuge for the Needy in Times of Distress

"O Lord, you are my God; I will exalt you and praise your name, for in perfect faithfulness you have done marvelous things, things planned long ago.

"You have been a refuge for the poor, *a refuge for the needy in his distress*, a shelter from the storm and a shade from the heat. For the breath of the ruthless is like a storm driving against a wall and like the heat of the desert.

"You silence the uproar of foreigners; as heat is reduced by the shadow of a cloud, so the song of the ruthless is stilled."

—Isaiah 25:1, 4–5 (NIV)

The hope expressed by Isaiah is beautifully mirrored in McNamara's observation,

Man's despair is not despair of God at all,
But despair of all that is not God.
Beyond that certain despair lies Christian hope.
—William McNamara[34]

Blessed be the God and Father of our Lord
Jesus Christ, who according
To His great mercy has caused us to be born again to a living hope
Through the resurrection of Jesus Christ from the dead.
—1 Pet. 1:3 (NASB)

"Bad-day, good-day theology" essentially asserts that if things are going well in my life, then God must love and care for me. However, if times are hard, and adversity strikes, then God must be off on a journey or tending to business in another part of the world, leaving me to struggle alone. In a moment of great pressure (bad day), the Hebrew youths did not question, rethink, or reinvent God, but instead they *revisited* what they knew to be true about Him. So, by a resounding affirmation that God is worthy to be trusted in the good days as well as in the bad times, they were able to withstand the pressure to relent and cave in to external pressures.

In a similar vein, Isaiah brings a word of comfort to the people of Judah when he reminds them that their God is both a mighty sovereign and the gentle shepherd of their hearts, transcendent yet tender (Isa. 40:9–11).

Likewise, Asaph the psalmist expressed his implicit trust in the immensity of God's gracious sovereignty in the following words, and by so doing, discovered heart-rest:

> "My flesh and my heart may fail…But as for me, it is good to be near God; I have made the sovereign Lord my refuge" (Ps. 73:26, 28 NIV).

How assuring to know that amidst those times when hearts are prone to fail, God, who inhabits eternity and indwells the most contrite and humble of hearts, not only delights to be our secure refuge, but has committed Himself to be constantly available to protect us from the crippling effects of disillusionment and unbelief.

Having freely made God his refuge, Asaph was not threatened by such an incredible relationship but rather was able to feel totally safe in God's awesome presence.

Perhaps you might ask why someone like the writer of the Psalms would need heart-rest. Surely, after having walked with and learned about God for so many years, you would think that he would have it all together, right? Well, as we have seen, not necessarily.

Like many of us, Asaph wrestled with some deep issues and questions that perplexed him. In particular, he asked,

- Why do the wicked prosper (Ps. 73:3)?
- What is the point of maintaining integrity when evil men ridicule it (Ps. 73:13)?
- Has God forgotten to be merciful (Ps. 77:7–9)?

Others Fought to Win the Prize[35]

> Must I be carried to the skies
> On flowery beds of ease,
> While others fought to win the prize
> And sailed through bloody seas?
>
> —Isaac Watts

> Precious in the sight of the Lord is the death of his saints
>
> —Ps. 116:15 (NIV)

Although Asaph did not have all of his questions fully and immediately answered, it is encouraging to see from Psalm 77 how he was able, nevertheless, to stay the course spiritually in the present by reflecting on how God had worked mightily on his behalf in the past. He said, "I will:

o   remember the deeds of the Lord,
o   meditate on all your works, and
o   consider all your mighty deeds" (Ps. 77:10–12 —NIV).

> Chip Ingram writes in his book, *I Am with You Always*, that the psalmist was able to focus more clearly on God's deeds when he specifically categorized them by *theological* (God's character), *historical* (God's involvement with the community of faith—Israel, etc.), and *personal* faith experiences (Ps. 77:10–12). By doing this, he was able to maintain great confidence in the Lord.[36]

In this regard, a friend of ours once commented, as she was recounting all of God's blessings in her life, "I should sit down and write a list of my blessings—it would be longer than the Great Wall of China!"[37]

The habit of remembering and meditating on key, faith-expanding experiences with God, as Asaph and our friend did, has been referred to as the celebration of "Memorial Stones of Remembrance" (Josh. 4:1–7; 1 Sam. 7:12), which signify the mighty work of God in our lives and reflects well the command in the Psalms where we read: "Forget not all his benefits" (Ps. 103:2 NIV).

As we consider and celebrate the various "memorial stones" of key, faith-expanding moments in our lives, we will be wonderfully reminded of the Lord's personal involvement (gracious oversight) in our lives. How blessed we are indeed to be able to recount for ourselves and others how the Lord has in mercy blessed us with displays of His most gracious intervention, help, abundant provision, perfect guidance, and protection.

In a practical way then, we may not only encourage ourselves but also others who follow our paths, by leaving, as Alexandra Johnson says, "a trace" of God's good hand in our journals and songs of praise.

So, if we desire to not remain unsettled by the relentless assaults of Satan, who seeks to ever dissuade us from further trust in God, then it is clearly important that we revisit often what we know to be true about God's person, power, and purposes. We can do this quite easily by reflecting on how the Lord has worked in and through our particular personal faith-expanding experiences and by consciously erecting high those significant memorial stones of God's working, which are the outflow from His abiding faithfulness, love, justice, goodness, and kindness.

Then Samuel took a stone and set it up between Mizpah and Shen.
He named it Ebenezer, saying, "Thus far has the Lord helped us."
—1 Samuel 7:12 (NIV)

Your Consolation

When anxiety was great within me,
Your consolation
brought joy to my soul.
—Psalm 94:19 (NIV)

One helpful way of meaningfully reflecting on and celebrating how God has worked in our lives is to journal (tracing out the *traces* or *handiwork*), which enables us to specifically take note of God's awesome character and the variety of ways He has ministered to us. The reader may find Chip Ingram's template (found on page 27) to be helpful in tracing out God's handiwork.

By revisiting what we know to be true about God's character and by increasing our awareness of His faithful ways, we come to discover that the key to entering and enjoying meaningful heart-rest, even if God appears to be silent, is to trust Him.

The psalmist wrote, "When I am afraid, I will trust in you" (Ps. 56:3 NIV).

Jeremiah said, "But blessed is the man who trusts in the Lord, whose confidence is in him" (Jer. 17:7 NIV).

Again, by choosing to affirm our implicit trust in the Lord's gracious, sovereign purposes and the integrity of His heart, we will discover an overarching composure and settled-ness of spirit, which in turn will still our troubled hearts amidst the harshest buffeting and most bewildering storms of life. The prophet Isaiah expresses this truth so perfectly when he writes: "Surely God is my salvation; I will trust and not be afraid. The Lord, the Lord, is my strength and my song; he has become my salvation" (Isa. 12:2 NIV).

Thankfully, there is a way out from the dreary, dark lands of disillusionment and a way forward to renewed vigor of faith in God's goodness. Yes, consternation and disillusionment with God and His ways are not our only options.

In Psalm 97:1, 9 we read, "The Lord reigns, let the earth be glad, let the distant shores rejoice. For you, O Lord are the Most-High over all the earth; you are exalted far above all gods" (NIV).

Commenting on this Psalm, Charles Spurgeon noted, "Causes for disquietude (anxiety) there are none, so long as this blessed sentence is true. On earth the Lord's power as readily controls the rage of the wicked as the rage of the sea; His love as easily refreshes the poor with mercy as the earth with showers."[38]

A Believer in Extremis[39]

O, Lord, do not forsake me; be not far from me, O my God.
—Psalm 38:21 (NIV)

In his study notes on Psalm 38, Greenslade observes that:

> This psalm describes a believer *in extremis*. He feels targeted by God's anger and displeasure (v.2). What a miserable condition he's in: bones out of joint, breath and sight failing, wounds festering ... this describes someone who is gravely ill ...
>
> Like Job, he suffers as a social outcast. But, unlike Job, this sufferer confesses his sin and admits his guilt ... Illness shuts down all your normal social senses (vv. 13–14). Being deaf to other voices, struck dumb of all self-serving rationalizations, the psalmist has only God to wait for (v.15). Only God will not forsake him in his crisis; only God will dare to come close to him (v.21). In the end ... he discovers that God Himself is our only saviour.

Should you, as a reader in a season of disillusionment, find that the urge to stop railing against God is increasingly more difficult and the hard, nagging questions (such as the ones below) continue to clamor for an answer … then don't lose heart!

❖ Why should the Lord even bother to attempt to bring good out of this awful tragedy?

❖ How can God possibly restore my soul to normalcy when all I can see on the horizon is this ongoing nightmare?

❖ Will He stay with me all the way through this darkest of valleys?

❖ Is it possible that any long-term healing can arise from such pain?

❖ Will I ever be able to trust again, and will my hope be renewed?

Remember, when we cannot see His hand, we can trust His heart, and *when there are no answers, then there are assurances*!

May the following affirmation of faith, composed by Johann Schutz, bring a settled calm to your anxious heart and troubled spirit, and bring renewed grace to your soul, as it has for many other friends:

> Sing praise to God who reigns above, The God of all creation,
> The God of power, the God of love, The God of our salvation;
>
> With healing balm, my soul He fills, And every faithless
> murmur stills: To God all praise and Glory!

—Johann Schutz[40]

THEOLOGICAL
HISTORICAL
PERSONAL

Until the Disaster Is Passed

Have mercy on me, O God, have mercy on
me, For in you my soul takes refuge.
I will take refuge in the shadow of your wings
Until the disaster has passed.
—Psalm 57:1 (NIV)

Part II
Daily Readings

My soul is downcast within me; therefore, I will remember you from the land of the Jordan, the heights of Hermon—from Mount Mizar.
—Psalm 42:6 (NIV)

When My Heart Is Overwhelmed

From the end of the earth will I cry unto thee, *when my heart is overwhelmed*; lead me to the rock that is higher than I.

For thou hast been a shelter for me, and a strong tower from the enemy.

I will abide in thy tabernacle forever; I will trust in the shelter of thy wings. Selah.

For thou, O God, hast heard my vows; thou hast given me the heritage of those who fear thy name.

Thou wilt prolong the king's life, and his years as many generations.

He shall abide before God forever; oh, prepare mercy and truth, which may preserve him.

So, will I sing praise unto thy name forever, that I may daily perform my vows.

—Psalm 61:2–8 (KJV)

Day 1—Drawing Strength from the Right Sources

> When my heart is overwhelmed; lead me
> to the rock that is higher than I.
> —Psalm 61:2 (KJV)

Have you ever experienced a season of *seeming* endless anguish of heart that has left you bewildered, overwhelmed, and numb? While long-term bewilderment arising from life's hardships can leave us reeling, possible disillusionment arising from God's *seeming* silence is more serious. Without a proper means for processing one's perplexity with the ways of Providence and the resultant distress from unresolved personal grief, disheartened souls may become embittered, or worse, grow to question if God cares, or even resent Him and thus draw conclusions about Him that are untrue and misleading.

Throughout the ages, many disheartened believers have found stability and hope amid bewildering circumstances by drawing their spiritual strength from the right sources. In *A Grief Observed*, C. S. Lewis wrote: "At first I am overwhelmed ... then I try to bring myself into the frame of mind I should be in at all times ... I become a creature consciously dependent upon God, drawing its strength from the right sources."[41]

The Bible introduces us to some of these people who found their spiritual strength in the right sources, people who did not need to rethink their view of God (or give up on him), because what they knew to be true of Him in the past fortified them with grace for the present. On the eve of King Nebuchadnezzar's assault on Jerusalem, Jeremiah revisited what he knew to be true about God and was thus enabled to affirm an unflagging faith in God, who promised to and eventually did bring about a great deliverance for His people. Read how the prophet drew his strength from the right sources as he focused on God's person, works, and awesome power.

Ah, Sovereign Lord, you have made the heavens and the earth by your great power and out-stretched arm. Nothing is too hard for you. You show love to thousands but bring the punishment for the father's sins into the laps of their children after them. O great and powerful God, whose name is the Lord Almighty, great are your purposes and mighty are your deeds. Your eyes are open to all the ways of men; you reward everyone according to his conduct and as his deeds deserve. You performed miraculous signs and wonders in Egypt and have continued them to this day. (Jer. 32:17–20 NIV)

❖ **Insight for Foresight**

"The problem of reconciling human suffering with the existence of a God, who loves, is only insoluble so long as we attach a trivial meaning to the word 'love', and look on things as if man were the centre of them. Man is not the centre. God does not exist for the sake of man."[42]

❖ **Moving on from Bewilderment and Anguish to Belief and Assurance**

As a helpful exercise, why not take a moment to list three well-known truths about God's character (attributes), which clearly represent for you the core underpinning of your understanding of who He is and why you trust in Him. Meditate on these truths and allow them to become an ongoing source of sustaining grace to your heart in this hour.

❖ **Leaving Our Questions and Pain in the Lord's Good Hands**

"Father, when my heart is overwhelmed, 'Lead me to the rock that is higher than I.' Yes, Lord, 'have mercy on Me, O God, have mercy on me, for in you my soul takes refuge. I will take refuge in the shadow of your wings until the disaster has passed'" (Ps. 61:2; 57:1 NIV).

Storms Are the Triumph of His Art[43]

Away despair! My gracious Lord doth Hear. Though Wind and Waves
Assault My Keel, He doth preserve it; He doth steer,
Ev'n when the boat seems to reel; *Storms are the triumph of His Art.* Well
may He close His eyes,
But not His heart.

—George Herbert

For He spoke and raised up a stormy wind, which lifted up
The waves of the sea. Then they cried to the Lord in their
Trouble, and He brought them out of their distresses.
—Ps. 107:25 & 28

Day 2—Revisiting What We Know to Be True about God

> He has besieged and encompassed me with bitterness
> and hardship. In dark places, he has made me
> dwell, like those who have long been dead.
> —Lamentations 3:5–6 (NASB)

When heavily burdened by the grief that had engulfed the survivors in Jerusalem, Jeremiah found that *by revisiting what he knew to be true about God,* he could keep himself from being carried away by what Charles Spurgeon called the *hurricanes of infidelity, which come from the wilderness.*[44] He wrote:

> I remember my affliction, the bitterness ... I well
> remember them, and my soul is downcast within me.
> Yet this I call to mind and therefore I have hope: because
> of the Lord's great love we are not consumed, for his
> compassions never fail ... the Lord is good to those
> whose hope is in him ... though He brings grief, he will
> show compassion, so great is his unfailing love (Lam.
> 3:19–22, 25, 32 NIV).

When life's mysteries defy explanation, believers can still find a clarifying ray of hope because they have recourse other than perplexity of mind and bitterness of heart. Like Jeremiah, we may revisit what we know to be true about God. Not having immediate answers can actually bring defining insights and assurances, in that we are constrained by faith to cast ourselves on the wisdom of God, who is infinitely wiser than we, and in whose Word of grace we find a stabilizing peace.

On different occasions, the psalmist would record how utterly indispensable the lifeline of God's Word was to him in times of suffering.

He wrote, "If thy word had not been my delight, then I would have perished in my affliction" (Ps. 119:92 NASB). On another occasion, he wrote, "Remember your word to your servant, for you have given me hope. My comfort in my suffering is this: Your promise preserves my life" (Ps. 119:49–50 NIV).

As the Holy Spirit directs our minds to revisit what we know to be true about God (Ps. 42:6) from his faithful Word, we are enabled to then draw strength from the right sources. As a result, we can maintain an eternal focus, even in the hour of a severe trial or momentary time of bewilderment.

❖ Insight for Foresight

"There is actually little comfort in thinking that God permits bad things to happen to good people because He is powerless to do otherwise. We may not understand the reason God allows some things to enter our lives, but we can always be confident that He is powerful enough to cope with them" (John Koessler).[45]

❖ Moving on from Bewilderment and Anguish to Belief and Assurance

To challenge yourself to a new and invigorating spiritual perspective on life during your next *quiet time,* why not spend a few moments of reflection on the collected wisdom of such gifted writers as: Augustine of Hippo, Jonathan Edwards, Charles Wesley, Dietrich Bonhoeffer, John Calvin, Blaise Pascal, George MacDonald, Andrew Murray, Charles Spurgeon, or C. S. Lewis.

❖ Leaving Our Questions and Pain in the Lord's Good Hands

"Gracious Lord, I thank you for the perfections of your Word, which continue to faithfully minister grace to my heart when I am hurting."

When the Mists Have Rolled Away[46]

by D. Sankey and A. H. Barker

1) When the mists have rolled in splendor, From the beauty of the hills,
And the sunlight falls in gladness, On the river and the rills,
We recall our Father's promise,
In the rainbow of the spray
We shall know each other better,
When the mists have rolled away.

Chorus:

We shall know ... as we are known ... Never more ... to walk alone ...
In the dawning of the morning,
Of that bright and happy day.
We shall know each other better
When the mists have rolled away.

2) Oft we tread the path before us
With a weary, burdened heart;
Oft we toil amid the shadows,
And our fields are far apart:
But the savior's "Come, ye blessed,"
All our labor will repay
When we gather in the morning
Where the mists have rolled away.

Chorus

3) We shall come with joy and gladness, We shall gather round the
     throne;
Face to face with those that love us,
We shall know as we are known;
And the song of our redemption
Shall resound through endless day,
When the shadows have departed,
And the mists have rolled away.

Chorus

Day 3—There Are Certainties Somewhere

For I consider that the sufferings of this present time are not
worthy to be compared with the glory that is to be revealed in us.
—Romans 8:18 (NASB)

Charles Haddon Spurgeon once wrote:

> It is well to make sure of what we know, for this will
> be a good anchor-hold for us when we are molested by
> those mysterious storms which arise from things we do
> not understand ... Experience has placed tangible facts
> within our grasp; let us then cling to these, and they will
> prevent our being carried away by those hurricanes of
> infidelity which still come from the wilderness.[47]

The question before us now is, are there certainties that will enable us
to draw strength from the right sources, certainties that will ensure that
we will not lose heart when we cannot understand the reasons for our
affliction and consequent anguished perplexity? Thankfully, the answer
is a resounding yes!

The apostle Paul expresses the believer's confidence during trials this
way: "I consider that the sufferings of this present time are not worthy
to be compared with the glory that is to be revealed in us" (Rom. 8:18).
By this he meant that we can be absolutely confident that the sheer
immensity of eternal glory will supersede all temporal grief. Such firm
conviction has merit in that it is confirmed in the experience of refined
believers and in God's Word. Second Corinthians 4:17 indicates that
afflictions are intended to be momentary in duration but monumental
in their design. The pain of momentary groaning is followed by the
perfection of a monumental glory in the end (Job 23:10). However, if we
are not careful, we can inadvertently switch the order of those words
amidst our pain, so that the experience appears to be one of monumental
pain, thus holding little, if any prospect for meaningful glory.

Does it not encourage you to see that the apostle Paul does not deny the reality of one's afflictions, as if they were simply a mere figment of our imagination, nor does he dismiss the trial of our faith as arbitrary happenstance or meaningless? Paul clearly acknowledges that though afflictions can be miserable, in the end they will be eclipsed by a monumental and enduring result of maturity. James wrote, "Let patience have her perfect work, that you may be mature and complete, lacking nothing" (James 1:4). In review, the divine purpose overarching our trials and the process of our perfection in Christ entails a *momentary* duration and a *monumental* design culminating in *mature* development ("being conformed to His image," Rom. 8:29 KJV). Yes, of these truths we can be certain!

❖ Insight for Foresight

"For the mountains may be removed and the hills may shake, but my lovingkindness will not be removed from you...says the Lord, who has compassion on you."[48]

❖ Moving on from Bewilderment and Anguish to Belief and Assurance

"Heaven, once attained, will work backwards and turn even that agony into a glory. And that is why, at the end of all things, *when the sun rises* here and the twilight turns to blackness down there, the blessed will say, 'We have never lived anywhere except in Heaven.'"[49]

❖ Leaving Our Questions and Pain in the Lord's Good Hands

"Father, thank you for the assurance that any momentary groaning associated with trials will be eclipsed by a monumental glory. Lord Jesus, may I today have your grace to allow patience to have its perfect work in my life, so I might be mature and complete *when the sun rises* in my eternal home."

Does Jesus Care?[50]

by F. E. Graeff

1) Does Jesus care when my heart is pained
Too deeply for mirth and song;
As the burdens press, and the cares distress, And the way grows weary and long?

Chorus

O yes, He cares—I know He cares! His heart is touched with my grief;
When the days are weary, the long nights dreary, I know my Savior cares.

2) Does Jesus care when my way is dark
With a nameless dread and fear?
As the day light fades into deep night shades,
Does He care enough to be near?

Chorus

3) Does Jesus care when I've tried and failed
To resist some temptation strong;
When for my deep grief I find no relief,
Tho' my tears flow all the night long?

Chorus

4) Does Jesus care when I've said good-bye
To the dearest on earth to me,
And my sad heart aches till it nearly breaks
Is it aught to Him? Does He see?

Chorus

Day 4—Making Sense of Things That Don't!

And we know that in all things God works
for the good of those who love him,
who have been called according to his purpose.
—Romans 8:28 (NIV)

Prior to receiving medical attention for extreme exhaustion, pop diva Mariah Carey told her fans, "I don't know what's going on with life. I'm trying to understand things in life."[51] Perhaps it would be fair to ask if Mariah was trying to make sense of things that did not?

Our world today would have us think that we are at the mercy of capricious whims of fate or karma (the sum total of a previous life's actions determining one's destiny in the next life) and that God has no interest in or any power over devastating catastrophes or natural disasters. Secular singers have reinforced this belief by telling us, "Que sera, sera; whatever will be, will be!"

When deep waters rise or sudden reversals in health or prosperity occur (Eccl. 9:12), and we find ourselves on the *unasked-for journey*, the Bible assures us that we may find consolation in Christ, knowing that with God in control of the universe, there is never a hint of anything being incidental or accidental in our life. Someone has said, "God is too-loving to be cruel and too wise to make a mistake!" Scripture affirms that as the objects of His eternal love and purpose, believers are not simply hapless pawns ensnared by the capricious whims of fate.

In Romans 8:28, we find a timeless balm of Gilead that has enabled God's people to endure when mysterious and bewildering events transpire in their lives: "We know that in all things, God works for the good of those who love Him, who are the called according to His purpose."

One may rightly ask, "So, what's the value of knowing that in all things God works for the good of those who love Him?" Citing Nietzche,

Nazi death camp survivor Viktor Frankel wrote, "He who has a *'why'* to live for, can bear with almost any *'how.'*"[52] In other words, people can cope with almost any mysterious misfortune if they believe there is a purpose behind it and a reason for it. Frankel believed that Jews who were not killed in the Nazi death camps found the strength to survive if they could fit their experience into a meaningful framework.

God's timeless Word is what enables believers today to understand the place for trials and suffering in their lives, by providing them with a meaningful framework for evaluating what is happening to them. When looking to Christ in the scriptures, believers are assured that life is not a cruel joke but rather a revelation of God on display at all times. Yes, when they suffer, they will come to know by experience that the conquering, comforting Christ is there to come alongside to minister overcoming grace (Rev. 1:9-18).

❖ **Insight for Foresight**

Like nothing else, standing at the coalface of adversity has a way of bringing into sharper focus the reality of God's tender mercies.

❖ **Moving on from Bewilderment and Anguish to Belief and Assurance**

One positive step in helping a believer to establish a proper framework for processing the reasons for suffering is to remember that God, who is good all the time, is in perfect control of all of life all the time and that the devil, who is evil all the time, remains subject to God Almighty all the time (Job 2)!

❖ **Leaving Our Questions and Pain in the Lord's Good Hands**

Thank you, gracious Lord, that you have promised that when we pass through the waters (Isa. 43:2), they will not overwhelm us and that in all of our distress, you are distressed (Isa. 63:9). Help me to trust you to bring about the desired good of your perfect purposes through all of life's pressures and troubles that distress my heart.

To Comfort All Who Mourn

The Spirit of the Sovereign Lord is on me …
To comfort all who mourn,
And provide for those who grieve in Zion—
To bestow on them a crown of beauty
Instead of ashes,
The oil of gladness
Instead of mourning,
And a garment of praise
Instead of a spirit of despair.

—Isaiah 61:1–3 (NIV)

Day 5—When We Cannot Change the Channel

> Elect ... according to the foreknowledge of God the Father.
> —1 Peter 1:1–2 (NIV)

Reflecting on the tragic death of Wycliffe missionary Chet Bitterman, a senior missionary director wrote, "When one stands between the Garden of Gethsemane and the cross, and the torches flicker in the deepening gloom, one needs to know who he is, what he is about and where his values lie."[53]

It should go without saying, but nevertheless, it is essential and helpful for Christians to know who they are, what they are about, and where their values lie in order to maintain a stabilizing spiritual perspective in an unsettling world that calls for uncommon graces for survival.

Several years ago, a cartoon depicted a frustrated father attempting to change a flat tire in the pouring rain. His children, unsettled by the delay, were peering out of a car window. In response to their complaints about the delay, the father said rather pointedly and wisely, "Don't you understand? This is life. This is what's happening. We cannot switch to another channel!"

In the first century AD, the apostle Peter wrote a message to exiled believers who were driven from their familiar roots and who had doubtless hoped for relief from the pressures of persecution. It would be understandable then to learn that they had longed to change the "channel" of their circumstances. In as much as Peter had understood that Christians had no assurance whatsoever of a continually-settled condition in this life, he directs his Christian friends to consider various biblical certainties, designed by God to provide internal stability of heart, thus enabling them to respond well in faith to the external upheavals associated with their circumstances.

The apostle Peter's message for this early band of faithful believers was simply this: "When you cannot switch the channel, you can still have God's unchanging grace for your appointed place in this world."

In particular, he reminded the Christians who they were in God's eyes by pointing out that they were, "elect according to the foreknowledge of God the Father." Therefore, in as much as they were rightly related to God as the elect of God (foreknown completely by God from eternity past), they could then properly evaluate their trials of faith in light of God's awesome omniscience and sovereign oversight of their lives, and thus find uncommon grace for survival.

What makes this truth even more significant is that God elected to save all who would believe in Jesus from the very moment His divine purposes were set in motion. "From the beginning, God chose you to be saved through the sanctifying work of the Spirit, and through belief in the truth. He called you to this through our gospel" (2 Thess. 2:13–14 NIV). If we cannot change the channel and we have to change the tire, thankfully, unchanging grace is as close as a change in focus from our momentary trials to eternal truths.

❖ **Insight for Foresight**

Believing that God has known us completely from eternity past brings stability and grace in spite of the world not wanting to know believers at all (Ps. 139:15)!

❖ **Moving on from Bewilderment and Anguish to Belief and Assurance**

"God rescues us not for our comfort but for our calling. God rescues us, not from physical suffering or death, but from spiritual defeat" Martin Ricquebourg.[54]

❖ Leaving Our Questions and Pain in the Lord's Good Hands

Heavenly Father, thank you for unchanging grace, which gives me complete security in Christ. I praise you that I have been accepted in the merit of the beloved One, known by you, even before I was in my mother's womb. Thank you for redeeming and calling me into blessed fellowship with you.

Therefore, I Have Hope

My splendor is gone and all that I had hoped from the Lord.
I remember my affliction and my wandering, the bitterness and the gall.
I well remember them, and my soul is downcast within me.
Yet this I call to mind, and *therefore I have hope*:
Because of the Lord's great love, we are not consumed,
For his compassions never fail.
They are new every morning; great is your faithfulness.
I say to myself, the Lord is my portion; therefore, I will wait for him.
The Lord is good to those *whose hope is in him*, to the one who seeks him;
It is good to wait quietly for the salvation of the Lord.
It is good for a man to bear the yoke while he is young.
Let him sit alone in silence, for the Lord has laid it on him.
Let him bury his face in the dust—*there may yet be hope.*
Let him offer his cheek to one who would strike him, and let him be
filled with disgrace.
For men are not cast off by the Lord forever.
Though he brings grief, he will show compassion, so great is His
unfailing love.
For he does not willingly bring affliction or grief to the children of men.
—Lamentations 3:18-33 (NIV)

Day 6—Exiled, Though Elect!

> They went about ... persecuted and mistreated ... the world was
> not worthy of them ... they wandered in deserts ... and in caves.
> —Hebrews 11:37–38 (NIV)

In Peter's first epistle, the apostle reminded the elect (those rightly related to God) but exiled from their familiar settings to assess who they were in Christ and how they were to relate to those about them. So then, how should Christians relate to those around them, especially when they encounter adverse circumstances and do not feel like acting like the elect? In a word, they are to consider themselves as those who are saved out of the world, separated from it, and sent back into it as ministers of grace. In this regard, Guinness wrote, "As we respond to the call of our Creator, we rise...to be the people He alone knows we are capable of being."[55]

To the exiled elect, Peter wrote, "To those who reside as aliens scattered throughout Pontus, Galatia, Cappadocia, Asia and Bithynia...May grace and peace be yours" (1 Pet 1:1-2 NASB). Christians, according to Peter, are viewed as sojourners (a noncitizen or foreigner) in this life; such awareness provides us with a key point of reference for knowing our place in this world.

The Greek phrase for a sojourner/resident-alien, *para epi demos*, is unique. It literally means to be sent to, or among the people as an exiled stranger. Christians who have been displaced from their familiar settings or comfort zones, because of ill health, financial reversals, or even persecution for the Gospel, may consider themselves at such a time as being divinely-selected alien-residents. Knowing that one has been placed in a particular circumstance by God's sovereign design (*to—among—people*) will enable him or her to reflect with authenticity, a sustainable hope, which only the living Christ can bring amid a seemingly insurmountable situation, or even to the hopeless themselves.

When the time comes for us to face persecution or mistreatment at the hands of a world system that is no friend to grace, and the torches being held in the hands of cold, calculating cynics flicker in the background (see yesterday's devotional), it's good to know for certain:

Who we are—that we have a *special calling*, a right relation to God by faith in Christ as the *elect* of God (1 Pet. 1:2), and furthermore: What we are about—that we have a *significant commission*, a right relation to humankind as *emissaries* of Christ (1 Pet. 1:1).

❖ Insight for Foresight

Possessing a special calling to bear the name of Christ in a spiritually-barren culture and environment is best understood to be seen as a casting amongst, and not as a casting aside. Instead of considering ourselves as abandoned aliens, we are ambassadors on assignment.

❖ Moving on from Bewilderment and Anguish to Belief and Assurance

In order to avoid despair or denial about life's trying circumstances, it may prove beneficial to cultivate instead a state of devotion for all of life (see Mary's example in John 11:32).

❖ Leaving Our Questions and Pain in the Lord's Good Hands

Father, should I ever find myself driven from my home, familiar settings, friends, or comfort zone, help me to remember that those with whom I come in contact may be alienated from you and may need a friend to lead them home to the shepherd of their souls.

God Will Take Care of You[56]

by W.S and C.D. Martin

Be not dismayed whatever be-tide, God will take care of you;
Beneath His wings of love abide, God will take care of you.

Chorus:

God will take care of you, Thru every day, O'er all the way; He
will take care of you, God will take care of you.

Thru days of toil when heart does fail, God will take care of you;
When dangers fierce your path assail, God will take care of you.

Chorus

All you may need He will provide, God will take care of you;
Nothing you ask will be denied, God will take care of you.

Chorus

No matter what may be the test, God will take care of you;
Lean, weary one, upon His breast, God will take care of you.

Chorus

Day 7—He Is There! He Is Aware! He Cares!

These things saith the first and the last, who was dead and is
alive ... fear none of those things which thou shalt suffer.
—Revelation 2:8, 10 (KJV)

In the winter of 1992 tragedy befell John Thompson, when farm
equipment severed his arms. Suppressing the pain as best as he could,
John staggered some 400 yards to his home, opened the doors with his
mouth and then called 911 with a pencil gripped between his teeth. The
brave, young boy surpassed his surgeon's hopes for recovery. Extensive
procedures were performed to restore his arms. Yes, with incredible
fortitude, he was enabled to survive the tragic ordeal to the utter
amazement of all who knew him. Words of encouragement came from
across America, as TV viewers followed the proceedings on the news.
In all, John received over $300,000.00 in donations, and heart-felt letters
from young and old.[57]

Those many sincere letters of support were a tremendous source of
inspiration for a person who had suffered greatly. When the Christians
in ancient Smyrna had experienced intense persecution and consequent
suffering for their faith, they were given a letter to encourage them
to persevere. This letter reminded them of the wondrous care God
through Christ gives to His followers who are wearied by contending
for righteousness and standing against evil.

In particular, the Lord Jesus revealed to the believers at Smyrna that He
is the conquering Christ, who is alive and alert to their affliction, and
the comforting Christ, who said in verse 10, "Do not be afraid!" His first
words were critical: "I am the first and the last." Similarly, this is how
Jesus described Himself to the apostle John in Revelation 1:17–18, where
we see Him as the conquering and comforting Christ.

What makes Jesus's words to John so significant is that he identifies
Himself as the "first and the last!" In Isaiah 44:6, we read that it is God

who utters these exact words. "Thus says the *Lord*, the *King* of Israel and his *Redeemer*, the *Lord of hosts*: I am the *first and the last*, and there is no *God* besides Me." Note the descriptive words above (in italics) so there can be no mistake as to the identity of the speaker. Jesus's claim that He is "the first and last" in Revelation 1 and 2 is a claim that only God Himself is entitled to make, thus assuring believers of the incredible truth that we may know the fullness of God's awesome presence in Christ when we suffer.

❖ Insight for Foresight

Job 23:10 (NIV), says, "But he knows the way that I take; when he has tested me, I shall come forth as gold!" What is the promise here? *I shall come forth!* We can cling to this assuring promise because it entails the prospect of a refined character and faith (Rom. 5:3–5; 1 Pet. 1:7).

❖ Moving on from Bewilderment and Anguish to Belief and Assurance

"When a tear is wept by you, do not think that God does not see; for, 'as a father has compassion on his children, so the Lord has compassion on those who fear Him.' Your sigh is able to move the heart of Jehovah; your whisper can incline His ear to you; your prayer can stay His hand; your faith can move His arm. Do not think that God sits on high taking no account of you. Remember that however poor and needy you are, yet the Lord thinks upon you" (C. H. Spurgeon).[58]

❖ Leaving Our Questions and Pain in the Lord's Good Hands

"Lord Jesus, thank you for drawing near to your own when they experience times of trouble, disillusionment, and uncertainty (Lk. 24:15). I am encouraged to know that you have known my soul in adversities (Ps. 31:7b KJV)."

Help, Lord!

Help, Lord, for the godly are no more; the faithful have vanished from among men.

Everyone lies to his neighbor; their flattering lips speak with deception.

May the Lord cut off all flattering lips and every boastful tongue that says, "We will triumph with our tongues; we own our lips—who is our master?"

Because of the oppression of the weak and the groaning of the needy, I will now arise, says the Lord. "I will protect them from those who malign them."

And the words of the Lord are flawless, like silver refined in a furnace of clay, purified seven times.

O Lord, you will keep us safe and protect us from such people forever.

—Psalm 12:1–7 (NIV)

I have Multiple Sclerosis and by God's Grace have experienced multiple kindnesses by my fellowman. God is taking away my pride and self-sufficiency and drawing me closer to Him. He continues to show His faithfulness and mercy to me.
—Charles Gaskill[59]

Day 8—A Refuge from Relentless Slander

> For consider Him, who has endured such hostility by sinners
> against Himself, so that you may not grow weary and lose heart.
> —Hebrews 12:3 (NASB)

Scandalous charges of lying or ulterior motives seem to be the norm in the political arena. Media personalities strain at gnats as they go toe-to-toe dissecting hints of inconsistency or moral failings of politicians. Likewise, guardians of the corridors of power tirelessly engage one another in attempts to do damage control in response to slurs against their charge's character or integrity.

Whether it's on the sport's field, in the political arena, the boardroom or court room, no one seems immune from the scourge of the tongue's poisoned barbs. If ever anyone was qualified to say that He had experienced the full-on effects and pain from slanderous tongues, undeserved verbal abuse, and profane blasphemy, it was the Lord Jesus.

- ❖ He was accused of having worked miracles in the name of Satan (Matt. 12:24).
- ❖ He was taunted to leave the cross to prove he was God (Matt. 27:40).
- ❖ He was insulted by criminals, who were condemned to die with him (Matt. 27:44).
- ❖ The Jews implied Jesus was illegitimate by saying, "We are not born of fornication" (Jn. 8:41 KJV).

In the book of the Revelation, the Lord Jesus comforts the Christians at Smyrna, who were troubled by verbal flailing from false, religious professors (2 Pet. 2:1–15 and Jude). He reminded them that He also had endured the same poisoned, slanderous barbs (Heb. 12:3; Jam. 3:8). Jesus said to them, "I know your afflictions … your poverty … *the slander* of those who say they are Jews …" (Rev. 2:9 NIV).

William Barclay summarizes how early Christians were slandered: "The words of the Last Supper—'this is my body,' and 'this cup is the New Testament in my blood' were taken and twisted into a story that the Christians sacrificed a child and ate the flesh. The Christians … spoke of the coming end of the world. Their slanderers took these words and twisted them into threats of being political and revolutionary agitators."[60]

It would seem that times have not changed. According to Gauthier, "Profaning Jesus Christ and Christianity still continues…Detractors of Christianity oppose us not by saying that we are wrong, but by saying that we are evil and dangerous."[61]

❖ Insight for Foresight

Dietrich Bonhoeffer noted, "To endure the cross is not a tragedy; it is the suffering which is the fruit of an exclusive allegiance to Jesus Christ."[62]

❖ Moving on from Bewilderment and Anguish to Belief and Assurance

"Blessed are those who are persecuted because of righteousness, for theirs is the kingdom of heaven. Blessed are you when people insult you and persecute you, and falsely say all kinds of evil against you because of me. Rejoice and be glad, because great is your reward in heaven, for in the same way they persecuted the prophets who were before you" (Matt. 5:10-12 NIV).

❖ Leaving Our Questions and Pain in the Lord's Good Hands

"Merciful Father, I find immense comfort in knowing that you have not disdained the suffering of the afflicted one, nor have you hidden your face from those who endure the assaults of the restless evil of a profane tongue (Ps. 22:24; Isa. 25:4–5)."

Even in These Dark Times[63]

A Zimbabwean Christian once requested:
"Pray for us, but do not pity us.
God is at work
Even, in these dark times."

Then all mankind fears—they tell what God has brought about
And ponder what He has done.

—Psalm 64:9 (ESV)

Day 9—No Southern Comfort This!

> Praise be to the God and Father of our Lord Jesus
> Christ, the Father of compassion and the God of all
> comfort, who comforts us in all our troubles.
> —2 Corinthians 1:3–4 (NIV)

A popular daily devotional once asked this question:

> Is there anything that can mend a broken heart? When
> unrelenting sadness darkens each day, or when grief
> overwhelms us, where can we find comfort and help?
> Can the human wisdom and care of friends, family or
> business associates provide the healing we need? As
> helpful as their encouragement and support may be,
> we soon discover that the inner ache of our soul is still
> there.[64]

In the New Testament book of 2 Corinthians 1, we are introduced to the God and Father of our Lord Jesus Christ. As God the Father, He is also the God of all comfort who upholds and sustains his children as they look to Him for strength of heart when afflictions threaten to overwhelm them. "For just as the sufferings of Christ are ours in abundance, so also our comfort is abundant through Christ" (2 Cor. 1:5 NASB). The word used in the original language to describe "troubles" (v. 4) is *thilipsei*. This word is sometimes translated: "distress or pressure." Essentially, *thilipsei* describes a condition in which such pressure is brought to bear on the believer that one feels as if he or she were a grape in a wine press being pressed beyond measure to endure. The apostle Paul encourages believers by reminding them that in times like these, the ever-present God Himself stills anxious, troubled hearts with His perfect peace and strength.

Furthermore, the Bible teaches that God's provision of comfort to believers during times of heavy burdens of heart and distress in the soul is the actual presence of the Holy Spirit or Comforter. In particular, substantial, lasting consolation that reaches deep into the fabric of a suffering believer's heart is the result of the unique working of the Holy Spirit. Yes, the comfort that God imparts goes beyond expressions of good cheer to the impartation of a strength of heart that has been brought in alongside of the one who is suffering (cf. Isa. 40:27–31). The Greek word for comfort (*paraklesis*) is similar to the familiar Greek word (*paraclete*), which denotes the ministry of the Holy Spirit, who comes alongside the believer as the Comforter.

❖ **Insight for Foresight**

God's merciful consolation is sufficient to uphold and carry us along, even when we lack the heart to endure (2 Cor. 1:8–10; 4:8–9). Regardless of the demands, pressures, distresses, troubles, or harassments, He remains the "God of all comfort, who comforts us in *all* our troubles" (2 Cor. 1:3–4 NIV).

❖ **Moving on from Bewilderment and Anguish to Belief and Assurance**

"We find thus by experience that there is no good applying to heaven for earthly comfort. Heaven can give heavenly comfort; no other kind. Earth cannot give earthly comfort either, as there is no earthly comfort in the long run" (C. S. Lewis).[65]

❖ **Leaving Our Questions and Pain in the Lord's Good Hands**

Lord Jesus, I thank you that you are, by your gracious Spirit, a very present help in seasons of heaviness of heart and distress of soul. I am comforted knowing that I am not alone in the hour of my sorrow, nor left alone to find strength of heart in the midst of my hurts.

Comfort Yourself[66]

As a mother comforts her child, so I will comfort you.
—Isaiah 66:13 (NIV)

Comfort yourself that you have an unchangeable, constant friend in Christ Jesus.

How excellent Jesus' friendship is. You may learn from His manner of treating His disciples on earth.

He treated them as a tender father treats his children; meekly instructing them, most friendly in conversing with them, and being ready to pity them, to help them, and to forgive their infirmities.

—Jonathan Edwards

Knowing that as you are sharers of our sufferings,
so also you are sharers of our comfort.
—2 Cor. 1:7

Day 10—An Enduring Consolation

> In our hearts, we felt the sentence of death. But this happened that
> we might not rely on ourselves but on God, who raises the dead.
>
> —2 Corinthians 1:9 (NIV)

Feodor Dostoevsky wrote, "I believe … suffering will be healed … in the world's finale, something so precious will come to pass that it will suffice for all hearts. It will comfort all resentments."[67]

Anyone who has suffered has eventually asked, "Why?" An important reason why God allows His people to endure suffering is found in 2 Corinthians 1:9–11. It would seem from these verses that God allows us to experience pressure beyond our *natural* means to withstand, so that we might appreciate through our *own* personal struggle the reality of the all-sufficiency of God's *supernatural* strength to bear us up.

German theologian J. P. Lange wrote, "Christians enjoy a three-fold fellowship: in suffering, in consolation and in prayer. Their life is derived from what Christ has suffered for them. This is the source of all their peace and strength, and this brings them into affectionate communion with Him…"[68]

The apostle Paul experienced the affectionate communion described by Lange, because he realized he could rely on God to provide overcoming strength through the presence of the Holy Spirit, irrespective of the nature of the affliction or pressure. He wrote that all comfort is available in all of our trials (2 Cor. 1:3–4, "all comfort … in all our troubles"). The point is clear: God's comfort is more than equal to offset the pressure of any trial that comes (cf. 2 Cor. 1:5, 7). The psalmist adds a very helpful insight when he writes, "Thou shalt increase my greatness, and comfort me on every side (Ps. 71:21 KJV)."

"Every side" suggests that God's comforting presence is all-encompassing irrespective of the type of need, time, or place.

Developing further the theme of "every side," we see that 2 Corinthians 1:10 is a classic example of the "every side" of God's comfort. Here we read: "He *has delivered* us from such a deadly peril, and he *will deliver* us. On him we have set our hope that he will *continue to deliver* us." One will note how the apostle Paul derived an enduring consolation not only from recalling the Lord's sure deliverances in the past, but also from an anticipation of His assured mercies in the present and future (Ps. 90:15).

❖ **Insight for Foresight**

The name of the Lord is a strong tower, where the righteous "can enter and be at rest even when all around and above is a sea of trouble" (Andrew Murray).[69]

❖ **Moving on from Bewilderment and Anguish to Belief and Assurance**

"I never encourage people to express their anger toward God. Tell Him of your pain, yes. Plead for mercy, surely. Pour out your heart to Him, with all its disappointments and sorrows and agonies and all the rest—certainly" (Luis Palau).[70]

❖ **Leaving Our Questions and Pain in the Lord's Good Hands**

"Father, the grandeur and vastness of your faithfulness is beyond comprehension, moving me to ascribe the highest praise possible to you in this hour—thank you."[71]

A Time to Tear and a Time to Mend

There is a time for everything,
And, a season for every activity under the heavens:
A time to be born and a time to die,
a time to plant and a time to uproot,
A time to kill and a time to heal,
a time to tear down and a time to build,
A time to weep and a time to laugh,
a time to mourn and a time to dance,
A time to scatter stones and a time to gather them,
a time to embrace and a time to refrain,
A time to search and a time to give up,
a time to keep and a time to throw away,
A time to tear and a time to mend ...
—Ecclesiastes 3:1–7 (NIV)

Day 11—Foundational Focus

When the foundations are being destroyed, what can the righteous do?
—Psalm 11:3 (NIV)

Growing up in Southern California, I occasionally found myself awakened during the night with earthquake tremors that left me feeling unsettled and wondering how safe I was. Obviously, I was too young at the time to appreciate the importance of solid and secure foundations for our house.

With treachery, injustice, and wickedness stalking his country's corridors of power and threatening to rend the very foundation of its soul and consequent spiritual stability, the psalmist cried out, "When the foundations are being destroyed, what can the righteous do?" (Ps. 11:3 NIV). The Lord's reply enabled the psalmist to see what God represented to him in that moment of distress and what *God Himself would do*, rather than what the *psalmist could do!*

In the next verse (11:4), God assures the writer with these words, "The Lord is in His holy temple." This indicates that God is present and accessible in all seasons as a refuge, even amidst unsettling times. God is in His holy temple, and "on His heavenly throne" (v. 4), signifying that our sovereign God will control the outcome of all distressing and unsettling national crises (cf. Hab. 2:20).

Convinced that God was present and in control, the writer concludes by saying, "Upright men will see his face" (v. 7). Such confidence shows that the gloom of present adversity need never eclipse our joy, nor obscure the prospect of God's intervention or our being with Him in glory forever. Is this not why the poet could say, "I'm never alone in the darkness, though nothing but trials I see. And though the furnace be seven times heated, the form of the fourth walks with me"?[72]

When disheartening events defy explanation and leave us unsettled, it is good to examine the foundational truths of our faith and to revisit what we know to be true about God. When the psalmist wrote, "If your law had not been my delight, I would have perished in my affliction" (Ps. 119:92 NIV), he meant that the truths of God's Word would keep us anchored to the rock of ages, so that the buffeting that assails our hearts, would not overwhelm our hearts in hard times (Eccl. 11:10; Mt. 7:24–27). What can the righteous do? The best thing for them to do is to stand still and see what God Himself will do: "Stand still [be firm] and you will see the deliverance the Lord will bring you today" (Ex. 14:13–14 —NIV).

❖ **Insight for Foresight**

"From every stormy wind that blows, from every swelling tide of woes, there is a calm, a sure retreat: T'is found beneath the mercy seat. Ah! Whither could we flee for aid, when tempted, desolate, dismayed: or how the hosts of hell defeat, had suffering saints no mercy seat."[73]

❖ **Moving on from Bewilderment and Anguish to Belief and Assurance**

A colleague of ours encouraged us long ago to remember often those friends in the Lord, who, by modeling the grace and integrity of Jesus, ever challenge us on to remain connected to God. This is a good time to think of ways of staying connected to God by drawing our spiritual strength from the right sources, such as through meditation on scripture and the emulation of Christ-like mentors. For further reflection, consider 1 Samuel 30:6 and Psalm 87:7b.

❖ **Leaving Our Questions and Pain in the Lord's Good Hands**

"Lord, save me!" (Matthew 14:30 NIV).

Children of the Heavenly Father[74]

by C. S. Berg

1) *Children of the heavenly Father*
Safely in his bosom gather;

> Nestling bird nor star in heaven
> Such a refuge e'er was given.

2) God his own doth tend and nourish,
In his holy courts, they flourish;

> Like a father kind he spares them,
> In his loving arms, he bears them.

3) Neither life nor death can ever
From the Lord his children sever,

> For his love and deep compassion
> Comforts them in tribulation.

> You have been my help; do not abandon me, nor forsake
> me, O God of My salvation! For my father and my
> mother have forsaken me, but the Lord will take me up.
> —Ps. 27:9-10 (NASB)

Day 12—Maintaining Normalcy in Free Fall

> Help, Lord, for the godly are no more; the faithful
> have vanished from among men.
>
> —Psalm 12:1 (NIV)

Gone are the days when people disputed whether there might be a frontal attack on, or an undermining of our world's fragile morality. James Reston of the *New York Times* wrote, "There is something in the air of the modern world: a defiance of authority, a contagious irresponsibility, a kind of moral delinquency, which is no longer subject to the restraints of religious faith or ethics. And these attitudes are now threatening not only personal serenity, but also public order in many parts of the world."[75] In light of Reston's observations, it's little wonder then that many maintain that a concerted effort has been made by secularism to not only ignore, but to rid modern society of all vestiges of biblical principles, morality or references to God in the public square.

As we saw yesterday, Psalm 11 is the anguished cry of one whose spirit has been sorely vexed by forces that have assaulted the foundations and integral fabric of his or her nation's values and security. With Psalms 10:13 and 12:1, 2, 8 referring more to the aggressive assault of the godless on the righteous, Psalm 11 relates more specifically to the unraveling of civility, ethics, morality, truth, and justice.

It is interesting that Psalm 11:3 does not ask what the *unrighteous* can do. This makes sense in that (from a biblical point of reference) they are the ones responsible for assaulting and deconstructing what is cherished by all who fear and follow God. By way of contrast, the righteous are very concerned about what can be done, hence the question, "what can the *righteous* do?" Practically speaking then, the essence of this question comes down to focusing on how we can maintain normalcy in free fall or balance amid life's turbulent stresses and demands.[76] Assured that security proceeds from stability in society and blessing flows from adherence to God's will, the righteous can forge ahead with confidence.

How pertinent then is Proverbs 29:2 where we read, "When the righteous thrive, the people rejoice; when the wicked rule, the people groan." So, what can the righteous do? Psalms 11-12 show that believers can do something beyond just contending for righteous standards (as vital as that is). In particular, we sense a call to activism, not in the political sense, but rather it is a call to actively appeal to God for help while celebrating the truth that God is in perfect control of the universe and world and that by reflecting on His exalted position in glory, we may enjoy a blessed heart-rest that stabilizes and sustains our spirits during times of emotional free fall.

❖ Insight for Foresight

"The violence which assails good men to test them, to cleanse and purify them, effects in the wicked their condemnation, ruin, and annihilation. Thus, the good man under pressure of affliction offers up prayers and praises. This shows that what matters is the nature of the sufferer, not the nature of the sufferings" (Augustine).[77]

❖ Moving on from Bewilderment and Anguish to Belief and Assurance

"You became imitators of us and of the Lord; in spite of severe suffering, you welcomed the message with the joy given by the Holy Spirit. And so, you became a model to all the believers in Macedonia and Achaia" (1 Thess. 1: 6–7 NIV).

❖ Leaving Our Questions and Pain in the Lord's Good Hands

"Heavenly Father, we come before you today to ask your forgiveness and seek your direction and guidance. We know your Word says, 'Woe to those who call evil good,' but that's exactly what we've done. We have lost our spiritual equilibrium and inverted our values. We confess that we have ridiculed the absolute truth of your Word and called it moral pluralism. We have worshipped other gods and called it multiculturalism." (Rev. Joe Wright).[78]

Be Merciful to Me, for I Am Faint

O Lord, do not rebuke me in your anger
or discipline me in your wrath.
Be merciful to me, Lord for I am faint;
O Lord heal me, for my bones are in agony.
My soul is in anguish. How long, O Lord, how long?
Turn, O Lord, and deliver me; save me because of your unfailing love.
—Psalm 6:1–4 (NIV)

Day 13—God Is Good at Any Time!

> I had fainted, unless I had believed to see the
> goodness of the Lord, in the land of the living.
> —Psalm 27:13 (KJV)

Playwright Archibald MacLeish created a play entitled *JB*. It was an attempt to put a modern spin on the book of Job. *JB* was written to question why God allows suffering in the world. MacLeish's anti-god bias is seen when Nicles, a Satan figure, wastes no time in trashing a revered Christian view of God by saying, "If God is God, he is not good; if God is good, then he is not God!"[79]

How refreshing then is the contrasting perspective of theologian Stephen Charnock, who wrote:

> The notion of goodness is inseparable from the notion of God. He is good, he is goodness, good in himself, good in his essence, good in the highest degree, possessing whatsoever is excellent, desirable; the highest good, because he is the first good; whatsoever is perfect goodness is God, whatsoever is truly goodness in any creature is a resemblance of God. All the names of God are comprehended in this one of *good*.[80]

The psalmist understood the importance of affirming his belief in the goodness of the Lord during difficult times. His comment "I had fainted" can be taken to mean: "I might have given in to despair, or I may have lost all heart to go on, had I not persevered in unwavering trust in the goodness of God to uphold and sustain me when my heart was overwhelmed" (see v. 14, "He shall strengthen thine heart" —KJV).

As the reader may well recognize, it has often been expressed in Christian circles that "God is good *all* the time!" Though true, the phrase has begun to possibly wear thin for some, owing to its overuse and our familiarity with it. As a possible optional phrase, I am equally comfortable with saying that *God is good at any time!* Yes, God is good all the time, but in particular, He is good at any time (which perhaps moves us closer to a specific focus)!

So, not only do we endorse that God *is*, but we affirm that six little words, *God is good at any time*, can make all the difference in our attitude to hardship, setbacks, and life's reversals, at any time!

❖ **Insight for Foresight**

During his visit to Molokai's leper colony, Robert Louis Stevenson wrote, "To see the infinite pity of this place, the mangled limb, the devastated face, the innocent sufferer smiling at the rod, a fool would be tempted to deny his God. He sees, he shrinks. But, if he gazes again, Lo beauty springs from the breast of pain."[81]

❖ **Moving on from Bewilderment and Anguish to Belief and Assurance**

"His goodness shines through in times when we are uncomfortable" (Gracia Burnham).[82]

❖ **Leaving Our Questions and Pain in the Lord's Good Hands**

"O my God, however perplexed I may be, let me never think ill of You. If I cannot understand you, let me never cease to believe in You. It must be so, it cannot be otherwise, You are good to those whom You have made good; and where You have renewed the heart, You will not leave it to its enemies" (C. H. Spurgeon).[83]

Where Jesus Reigns

Where Jesus reigns there is no fear, No restless doubt, no hopeless tear,
No raging sea, nor tempest dread, But quietness and calm instead.
—Anonymous

Day 14—Confident in God's Unalterable Goodness

> I would have despaired unless I had believed that
> I would see the goodness of the Lord
> in the land of the living.
> —Psalm 27:13 (NASB)

Yesterday we began a consideration of Psalm 27:13. As we continue to reflect on the psalmist's affirmation of the goodness of God, it is noteworthy that the emphasis in this verse is not on the need to adopt an optimistic outlook about life. Instead, it is about focusing on the essential goodness of God's awesome character. See how the writer of this psalm was persuaded that God's goodness would never be eclipsed by the terrors and taunts of God's enemies (v.12). Rather, he was enabled to persevere with unflinching resolve of heart by being confident that God would manifest His sustaining grace and mercy during his lifetime.

When assailed by doubts and pressures from Satan to assume that all was beyond hope, and that God was remote and unconcerned about his welfare, the psalmist gave evidence of a deep and abiding faith in the goodness of God by writing, "I would have despaired unless I had believed that I would see the goodness of the Lord in the land of the living" (Ps. 27:13 NASB).

To have said, "I would have despaired (fainted or lost heart), had I not believed," is similar to saying, "I would have collapsed financially, had I not invested early on," or, "I would have been bumped from my flight, had I not confirmed the reservation," or, "I would have lost my soybean crop, had I not sprayed with pesticides before the latter rain," all of which are understandably essential actions.

Commenting on human suffering and the goodness of God, the Moody Bible Institute's devotional, *Today in the Word*, reminds us, "Obviously, it matters what you believe about the goodness of God and the way He deals with people.

As much as human logic might make us think otherwise, God's goodness is not on trial for human suffering. Instead, the issue is the outworking of His purpose."[84]

Understanding how vital it is to have a solid belief system in place early in life, the Chinese have a proverb that enjoins us to "dig a well, before you're thirsty." Even King Solomon used a similar line of practical (divine) wisdom when he said toward the end of his life, "Remember your creator in the days of your youth, before the days of trouble come ... and you will say, 'I have no pleasure in them'" (Eccl. 12:1 NIV). So, having taken care to establish the primacy of commitment to an unwavering belief in the goodness of God, we will find the requisite strength of heart to withstand assaults on our faith.

❖ Insight for Foresight

"I clearly recognize that all good is in God alone, and that in me, without divine grace there is nothing but deficiency" (Catherine of Genoa).[85]

❖ Moving on from Bewilderment and Anguish to Belief and Assurance

"'Truly God is good to Israel' (Ps. 73:1 KJV). He is only good, nothing else but good to his own ... he cannot act unjustly to them; his goodness to them is beyond dispute, and without mixture. To such he is, and must be goodness itself. The psalmist *does not doubt* this, but lays it down as his firm conviction" (Charles Haddon Spurgeon).[86]

❖ Leaving Our Questions and Pain in the Lord's Good Hands

Lord, we rejoice in our hope that *goodness and mercy shall pursue (overtake) us all the days of our life and that we shall dwell in the house of the Lord forever.* May it please you to encourage all who are disheartened, who stagger about with seeming unbearable burdens, by imparting an unswerving resolve to trust in your unfailing goodness.

To Whom Will You Compare Me?

"*To whom will you compare me*? Or, who is my equal?" says the Holy One.

Lift your eyes and look to the heavens: Who created all these? He, who brings out the starry host one by one, and calls them each by name. Because of his great power and mighty strength, not one of them is missing.

Why do you say, O Jacob, and complain, O Israel, "My way is hidden from the Lord; my cause is disregarded by my God?"

Do you not know? Have you not heard? The Lord is the everlasting God, the creator of the ends of the earth. He will not grow tired or weary, and his understanding no one can fathom.

He gives strength to the weary, and increases the power of the weak.

Even youths grow tired and weary, and young men stumble and fall;

But those who hope in the Lord will renew their strength. They will soar on wings like eagles; they will run and not grow weary, they will walk and not be faint.

—Isaiah 40:25–31 (NIV)

Day 15—A Cure for Weariness of Heart

> For the Lord is a God of justice. Blessed are all who wait for him.
> —Isaiah 30:18 (NIV)

Habakkuk, an Old Testament prophet, once lamented, "Justice is perverted" (Hab. 1:4 NIV). The father of the accuser in the highly-publicized Kobe Bryant sex scandal trial wrote to the judge saying he did not believe justice would be served in the criminal hearings, and threatened to move to a civil plea.

Whether we will ever see true, lasting justice carried out in our lifetime is an oft-repeated concern of heart and theme in literature. Augustine of Hippo gives us cause for hope when he states,

> It often happens that God shows more clearly His manner
> of working in the distribution of good and bad fortune.
> For if punishment was inflicted on every wrongdoing in
> this life, it would be supposed that nothing was reserved
> for the last judgment; on the other hand, if God's power
> never openly punished any sin in this world, there would
> be an end to belief in providence.[87]

Many of us know the promises in Isaiah 40:27–31 (for power and strength of heart). However, I sense that we may appreciate better the significance of these promises when we learn that the key word in the passage is "weary." Can you imagine why the people of Israel were weary? Isaiah 40:27–31 was written because God's people were weary of seeing and experiencing widespread injustice, and of wondering if they would ever see the justice of their cause upheld. Though the Bible tells us that God cares deeply about justice being upheld (Isa. 30:18), He is equally concerned about the effect injustice may have on our attitudes (lest we succumb to unfettered cynicism), and whether we can still believe that He will eventually judge all evildoers.

The truth is God is so concerned about upholding justice that He personally comes alongside His own people who are wearied by the reality of injustice to encourage them. God does not tell His weary people to visit their lawyer or therapist (as helpful as these two individuals may be on various occasions). Instead, He invites them to affirm their belief that God is a God of justice and to believe that the judge of all the earth will do right (Gen. 18:25). For more insight on God's heart for justice, read: Isaiah 9:7; 11:3–4; 32:1; 51:4; 56:1. Thankfully, Jesus tells us that the Lord "will see that they (his own) get justice, and quickly" (Lk. 18:7–8 NIV).

❖ **Insight for Foresight**

"Still less do I endorse the current idea that we can 'forgive' God, as though we were the judge and He the sinner. These are horrendous, even blasphemous ideas. Rather, we should fall on our faces and say, 'God, have mercy on me!'" (Luis Palau).[88]

❖ **Moving on from Bewilderment and Anguish to Belief and Assurance**

"I need Thee every hour, most gracious Lord; No tender voice like Thine can peace afford.

I need Thee every hour, Stay Thou nearby; Temptations lose their power When Thou art nigh.

I need Thee every hour, in joy or pain; Come quickly and abide, or life is vain" (Annie S. Hawks).[89]

❖ **Leaving Our Questions and Pain in the Lord's Good Hands**

"Heavenly Father, you commended the childlike faith of the persistent widow who petitioned the unjust judge to rule in her favor. Lord, may you uphold now the cause of your child, lest weariness overwhelm her spirit."

In All Their Distress

In all their distress he too was distressed, And the angel of his presence saved them. In his love and mercy, he redeemed them; He lifted them up and carried them all the days of old.
—Isaiah 63:9 (NIV)

Day 16—The Judge of All the Earth Will Do Right

> Will not the judge of all the earth do right?
> —Genesis 18:25 (NIV)

> You have seen, O Lord, the wrong done to me. Uphold my cause!
> —Lamentations 3:59 (NIV)

Bill Bright, founder and late president of Campus Crusade for Christ (Cru), emphasized the importance of maintaining a correct understanding of God's character and attributes during the storms of life. He wrote, "Life makes sense when God does!"[90]

When injustice brought dismay to his heart, the prophet Jeremiah went to the right sources to draw sustainable, spiritual strength. In particular, he reflected on the integrity of God's character and His awesome attributes. As a result, Jeremiah was assured that life could make sense, knowing God, who does make sense and who cares about his people's struggles. In Lamentations 3:19–33, we read about the confidence Jeremiah had in God's care and, by way of application, what we also may enjoy because of God's *great love* (v. 22), *his faithfulness* (v. 23), *his goodness* (v. 25), and because *he does not willingly bring grief to the children of men* (v. 33).

From this passage of scripture, we see that Jeremiah was confident in God's care for him personally. He was also convinced of the absolute comprehensiveness of God's justice for all humankind. In verses 34–36, he lists violations against human dignity that the Lord will never disregard. In particular, Jeremiah cites the mistreatment of prisoners (v. 34), the denial of basic human rights (v. 35), and the repealing of justice (v. 36). How encouraging to know that God also regards our pleas for comprehensive justice.

In his concluding remarks in Lamentations 3, Jeremiah himself shows us what we may expect when we adopt his approach to offsetting dismay over life's injustices. When Jeremiah called on the Lord in prayer ("I called on your name, O Lord, from the depths of the pit" [Lam. 3:55]), he affirms that:

- God heard the plea—v. 56   —Compare with 1 Peter 3:12; Ps. 18:6.
- God came near—v. 57   —Compare with Luke 24:15; Rev. 1:17–18.
- God took up the cause—v. 58   —Compare with Luke 18:7–8.
- God saw the wrong—v. 59, 60   —Compare with Psalm 106:44.
- God heard the insults—v. 61   —Compare with Isaiah 63:9.
- God will mete out justice—v. 64   —Compare with Psalm 75:2.

❖ Insight for Foresight

"How did Jesus control Himself, when scoundrels, whose very lives He sustained, spit in His face? Jesus had faith in the future grace of God's righteous judgment" (John Piper).[91]

❖ Moving on from Bewilderment and Anguish to Belief and Assurance

Thankfully, the Lord Jesus showed believers by His example the importance of drawing spiritual strength from the right sources. To know personally the composure of Christ amidst our struggle with injustice, the Bible exhorts us to model Christ's example by anticipating with assurance God's future grace. The apostle Peter reminds us, "While suffering, He (Jesus) uttered no threats, but kept entrusting himself to Him who judges righteously" (1 Pet. 2:23).

❖ Leaving Our Questions and Pain in the Lord's Good Hands

"Gracious heavenly Father, righteous judge of the whole earth, thank you for John Bunyan's advice: 'Hast thou escaped? Laugh. Art thou taken? Laugh. I mean, be pleased, which way so-ever things shall go, for that the scales are still in God's hand.'"[92]

Rejoicing in Suffering

And we rejoice in the hope of the glory of God. Not only so, but *we also rejoice in our sufferings*, because we know that suffering produces perseverance; perseverance, character; and character, hope. And hope does not disappoint us, because God has poured out his love into our hearts by the Holy Spirit, whom he has given us.

—Romans 5:2–5 (NIV)

Day 17—Exerting a Full-Court Press on Our Frets

Do not fret because of him who prospers in his way.
—Psalm 37:7 (NASB)

Psalm 37 speaks to our common tendency to fret over what appears to be endless injustices perpetrated by the wicked who enjoy prosperity while the righteous languish in poverty and adversity. Frets are those internal responses to things that may cause sustained uneasiness or an exasperated state of mind. When we are given to fretting, we not only become agitated, but we also can experience a vexation of spirit, or what Shakespeare calls the "1000 natural shocks that the flesh is heir to."[93]

Why should a Christian avoid fretting? In that fretting may lead one to focus on what is typically beyond one's control, fretting may end up wearing one down emotionally. Fretting can also distort our perspective, in that it influences us to see things as they appear to be, instead of seeing things as they really are (from God's perspective—see Ps. 37:12–15). In that the psalmist was concerned that the temporal groaning associated with fretting might deprive one of eternal graces, he exhorts his readers to stop fretting or becoming dismayed in mind, because of the distinct danger of forfeiting God's gracious gift of perfect peace. To enable one to begin to overcome the tendency to fretting, the psalmist gives us some practical steps in Psalm 37:1–8. These may be likened to a full- court press, which is often employed by a basketball coach as a defensive strategy to pressurize and frustrate an opponent's offensive strategy.

Avoid the inordinate preoccupation of attempting to right wrongs that are out of our control by adopting a "faith focus," which helps us to see things from God's eternal perspective, in contrast to a "fret focus," or humankind's temporal view point (vv. 1–2).

Absorb yourself with God's stabilizing peace by fully trusting Him, instead of fretting and fuming. This is sensible, in as much as impatience inflames exasperation, leading to a lack of trust in God's ways (vv. 3–4).

Assess not just the present but also the future (don't look around, but rather look ahead). Verse 10 says, "In a little while, the wicked will be no more." If the long view is the answer to righting wrongs, we can afford to await God's timing in the present (v. 5).

Anticipate that God will bring about a good result when we trust Him to work in us and to perfect those things that concern us. Philippians 1:6 reminds us, "He, who began a good work in you, will carry it on to completion until the day of Christ Jesus" (v. 7).

Assume a posture of settled-assurance instead of self-assertion. Believers may be assured that we are ever in God's hands (Jn. 10:28) and that God is with us (v. 8 & 18).

❖ **Insight for Foresight**

"By the grace of God I never fret, I repine at nothing. I am discontented with nothing. And to hear persons at my ear fretting and murmuring at everything is like tearing the flesh off my bones" (John Wesley).[94]

❖ **Moving on from Bewilderment and Anguish to Belief and Assurance**

"When God is in clear focus, His powerful presence eclipses our fears" (Chuck Swindoll).[95]

❖ **Leaving Our Questions and Pain in the Lord's Good Hands**

I thank you, Lord Jesus, for the assurance that, "God is God; He sees and hears all our troubles, all our tears. Soul, forget not, 'mid thy pains God o'er all forever reigns."[96]

It Is Well with My Soul[97]

by Horatio Spafford

1. When peace, like a river, attendeth my way, when sorrows like sea billows roll.

   Whatever my lot, thou hast taught me to say, It is well, it is well with my soul.

Chorus

   It is well with my soul, it is well, it is well with my soul.

2. Tho Satan should buffet, tho trials should come, Let this blest assurance control,

   That Christ hath regarded my helpless estate, And hath shed His own blood for my soul.

Chorus

3. My sin—O the bliss of this glorious thought—My sin, not in part, but the whole,

   Is nailed to the cross, and I bear it no more: Praise the Lord, praise the Lord, O my soul!

Chorus

4. And Lord, haste the day when my faith shall be sight, the clouds be rolled back as a scroll:

   The trump shall resound and the Lord shall descend, Even so— it is well with my soul.

Chorus

Day 18—Into Your Presence I Come

> I looked and behold, a door standing open in heaven.
> —Revelation 4:1 (NASB)

Norman Everswick was a godly pioneer missionary who served the Lord faithfully in Africa for forty years. After his memorial service, one of his granddaughters spoke with a man who is responsible for investing billions of US dollars. She said, "I do not think my grandfather left any material, earthly goods. However, he did leave us a great example of what it means to be godly, and that is invaluable. We will not forget, because we have been blessed!" Today, Norman Everswick lives on, not only as a spiritual giant in our memories (Ps. 112:6), but in the fullness of joy, celebrating the glorious liberty of the sons and daughters of God in the incomparable perfections of heaven. How apt then a comment from one of his sons who said rather poignantly, "Dad is where he was created to be. He is with the Lord, and we will see him again."

When the apostle John was imprisoned for his faithfulness to the Gospel, he received words of grace from the Lord that enabled him to look beyond his momentary affliction on earth to the eternal joys awaiting him in heaven. In Revelation 4, we find the following inspiring words of grace:

❖ Giving us *confidence*—"A door standing open in Heaven"—Revelation 4:1 (cf. Acts 7:56).

Jesus is the ladder between heaven and earth, granting access to God—John 1:51; Heb. 10:19–20.
Jesus goes before us to prepare a place in heaven—John 14:1–3.
Jesus is the way to the Father and the door to heaven—John 10:9; John 14:6.

❖ Inviting us to enjoy *communion* with God—"Come up here!"—Revelation 4:1.

Jesus desires intimate fellowship with His followers—John 14:23; Revelation 3:20.

Jesus promises to reveal or manifest Himself to us (share His heart)—John 14:21.

❖ Showing us that God is in *control*—"A throne"—Revelation 4:2.

With Jesus on the throne of God, we know He is in control of our lives—Revelation 4:11 & 5:13.

God's throne is not only a throne of authority and glory, but a throne of grace to which we may come to find grace and mercy to help us in times of need (Heb. 4:14–16).

Revelation 4 is a word of grace, reminding us that our sovereign God cares for us so much, that He has taken the initiative to communicate with us and to comfort us by lifting our gaze beyond immediate trials to the unshakable certainty of eternal hope, rest, and glory in heaven.

❖ **Insight for Foresight**

"The thing that ought to cause the heart to beat more rapidly is to live in the expectation that God will provide us with a fuller disclosure of the wonder of the Son of God" (Oswald Chambers).[98]

❖ **Moving on from Bewilderment and Anguish to Belief and Assurance**

"But maturing believers realize that heaven is much more than a destination. Heaven is a *motivation*."[99]

❖ **Leaving Our Questions and Pain in the Lord's Good Hands**

"Lord, thank you that one day the blessed hope will be a present reality. Today, however, we praise you for the comfort and motivation of a living hope that Christ imparts, inspiring us to live for and serve you faithfully, while keeping our eyes on our eternal reward and destination."

When We Cannot Fly Away and Be at Rest

Listen to my prayer, O God, Do not ignore
my plea; Hear me and answer me.
My thoughts trouble me and I am distraught
At the voice of the enemy,
At the stares of the wicked;
For they bring down suffering upon me, and
Revile me in their anger.
My heart is in anguish within me;
The terrors of death assail me.
Fear and trembling have beset me;
Horror has overwhelmed me.
I said, "Oh, that I had the wings of a dove!
I would fly away and be at rest—
I would flee far away
And stay in the desert;
I would hurry to my place of shelter,
Far from the tempest and storm."
Cast your cares on the Lord
And He will sustain you;
He will never let the righteous fall.
—Psalm 55:1–8; 22 (NIV)

Day 19—Beyond Grin and Bear It

> Strengthened with all power, according to His glorious
> might for the attaining of all steadfastness and patience.
> —Colossians 1:11 (NASB)

Toward the conclusion of J.R.R. Tolkien's *The Two Towers*, we find the intrepid heroes Frodo and Sam preparing to enter the dreaded land of Mordor. Having discovered their quest to be increasingly more dangerous than they had initially conceived and finding no alternative but to persevere, they decide to press on, more intent than ever in their quest to destroy the Ring of Power. The turning point in their deliberations, which enabled them to renew their determination to complete their epic venture, seemed to be when Sam told Frodo about the heroes of the great stories of old. At one clarifying moment as they struggled within themselves, Sam said, "The brave things in the old tales and songs, Mr. Frodo...I used to think that they were things the wonderful folk of the stories went out and looked for...but that's not the way of it with the tales that really mattered...I expect they had lots of chances, like us, of turning back, only they didn't."[100]

In 2 Timothy 2:3–6, we read about individuals who model steadfast endurance, because they hold onto certain convictions, expectations, and hopes amidst their respective hardships and challenges, and thereby, do not turn back.

❖ A farmer endures until the completion of the harvest.

❖ A soldier endures until he or she is discharged or victory is won.

❖ An athlete endures to the completion of his or her race (1 Cor. 9:24).

❖ A believer endures hardship in order to bring others to salvation (2 Tim. 2:10, 12).

Note how each of the above individuals has a distinct reason for life and receives a reward and an appropriate recognition for faithfully enduring and completing his or her assigned calling in life.

Endurance may then be defined as a steadfast, plodding resolve of heart to complete a task. Eugene Peterson develops the theme of endurance in his book entitled, "A Long-Term Obedience In the Same Direction."[101] The idea behind the grace of enduring is not just about holding on (as vital as that is) but in *holding firm* to a set course.

So, it may prove helpful to view endurance not simply from the perspective of a "grin and bear it" tenacity but rather, as one author puts it, "a call to a creative redirecting of less than desirable circumstances." This will enable us to discover by faith greater depths to God's grace.

❖ Insight for Foresight

It would seem that the act of expressing a *future* trust in God is not as difficult as encouraging the formation of a *further* trust in Him. In other words, few, if any, believers would doubt they have faith in God to save them and keep them for heaven *(future trust)*, whereas many find themselves struggling with allowing Him to direct all of life's daily decisions *(further trust)*.

❖ Moving on from Bewilderment and Anguish to Belief and Assurance

Sadly, many who have ceased to fight the good fight of faith often fail to discover more of the faithfulness of God. Accrued spiritual wisdom confirms that if we do not endure by a continual exercise of faith in Christ, then we run the risk of undermining our growth in grace, grieving the Spirit of God, and short-circuiting mature spiritual development (Heb. 5:14).

❖ Leaving Our Questions and Pain in the Lord's Good Hands

"Lord, may I have grace to persevere, as Moses, who 'saw Him who is invisible' (Heb. 11:27 NIV)."

Heralds of Weighty Mercies[102]

> It is a blessed thing, that when we are most cast down, then it is that we are most lifted up by the consolations of the Spirit, because trials make more room for consolation ...
>
> The humbler a man lies, the more comfort he will always have, because he will be more fitted to receive it ... Come troubled believer, fret not over your heavy troubles, for they are the *heralds of weighty mercies.*
>
> —Charles Haddon Spurgeon

And since we have a great high priest over the house of God, let us draw near with a sincere heart in full assurance of faith.

—Heb. 10:21-22 (NASB)

Day 20—Grace Guidelines for Endurance

> For you have need of endurance, so that when
> you have done the will of God,
> You may receive what was promised.
> —Hebrews 10:36 (NASB)

If we bear in mind the common distractions to endurance and how we might be adversely influenced by them, we will be better equipped to endure adversity and hardship. Here are some examples of known distractions that threaten to impede our endurance as believers.

- Looking at ourselves too often (knowing our own propensity to falter).
- Looking at obstacles too long (knowing the power of the world, the flesh, and the devil).
- Looking at opposition too anxiously (knowing how relentlessly powerful a secular culture is).

Hebrews 10:32–39 outlines four grace guidelines for enabling us to endure well in life.

❖ *Recall*: (v. 32) If the great cloud of witnesses referred to in Hebrews 12:1 refers to the faithful company of believers (Heb. 11), who stand as a testimony to God's faithfulness to enable believers to endure to the end, then we may also find grace to endure by looking back to those moments when God *enabled them* (and ourselves) to stand firm. "Remember when you stood your ground in a great contest in the face of suffering." Finding encouragement from the example of those who were enabled by God to endure in the past, believers today may find grace to endure faithfully to the end as well.

❖ *Rehearse*: (v. 35) Our surpassing confidence in Christ carries with it the promise of a great recompense and an inheritance that can never perish. Sadly, adversity or antipathy can erode the wonder of such a prospect.

One author suggests that our confidence can be eroded "not by one giant step, but in many shuffles." To provide a safeguard against adverse influences bent on eroding the wonder of our privileged position in Christ, the author of Hebrews proposes that we are not to treat our inheritance lightly, but that we are to rehearse in our hearts what the incredible blessing of knowing Him means to us.

❖ *Rely*: (v. 37–38) A college classmate arrested my attention when he said, "When faith is most difficult, it is most necessary!"[103] Much has been written about the indispensable role of faith in a believer's walk. Jesus commends great faith (Matt. 8:10) and is concerned by the lack of it (Lk. 18:8). The writer of Hebrews understood that if we are to endure, we must continue living by faith in God (Heb. 10:38).

❖ *Realize*: (v. 38–39) Not only are believers to realize the need for patient endurance (v. 36), but the author of Hebrews also reminds us that there are monumental consequences for not esteeming God worthy of further trust. This is a good time to list those particular areas where we struggle to let go and allow Jesus to direct our affairs.

❖ **Insight for Foresight**

"God hath seen mine affliction and the labour of my hands."[104]

❖ **Moving on from Bewilderment and Anguish to Belief and Assurance**

"Endure hardship with us as a good soldier of Christ Jesus" (2 Timothy 2:3 NIV).

❖ **Leaving Our Questions and Pain in the Lord's Good Hands**

"Thank you, Father, for your Son, Jesus, who endured the hostility of sinners and continued to do good to the end."

Fundamentally Weakened[105]

Over two thousand years ago, the apostle Paul reminded the believers in Corinth that he had personally experienced what he termed "the sentence of death," so that he would not trust in himself, but in God who raises the dead (2 Cor. 1:9).

Though separated by two millennia, Watchman Nee expressed perfectly Paul's words, when he stated, God must bring us to a point—I cannot tell you how it will be, but he will do it—where, through a deep and dark experience, our natural power is touched and *fundamentally weakened*, so that we no longer dare trust ourselves.

—Watchman Nee

> Therefore I am well content with weaknesses, with insults, with distresses, with persecutions, with difficulties for Christ's sake; for when I am weak, then I am strong.
> —2 Cor. 12:10a (NASB)

Day 21—Spinning Barrel Realities

Standing firm in one spirit … stand firm in the Lord, my beloved.
—Philippians 1:27; 4:1 (NASB)

One day, Charles Spurgeon and a friend attended a country fair. One of the attractions was a large, spinning barrel through which contestants attempted to walk without falling. Having purchased a ticket, Mr. Spurgeon accepted the challenge of walking through the barrel as it spun, and as it turned out, he was successful in his first attempt to walk through without falling over. His friend followed but faltered and tumbled down. Upon regaining his footing, Spurgeon's friend asked him, "How did you do that?" With an upraised finger, Spurgeon replied, "I kept my eyes fastened on the mirror hanging on that tree over there, just beyond the barrel."[106]

God's Word tells us how we may stand firm (not still), resolute and undeterred in our encounter with the spinning-barrel realities of life. One helpful way of standing firm is to view life through the lens (the mirror) of God's sovereign agenda. Over the years, I have discovered that whenever I have needed some clarifying perspective during the baffling experiences of life, I could always turn to the apostle Paul's words and find grace to stand firm. He wrote, "What has happened to me has really served to advance the gospel," and "What has happened to me *will turn out* for my deliverance" (Phil. 1:12, 19).

Now, notice for a moment Philippians 1:13 in light of Philippians 1:12 and what Paul did not say. He did not say he was in chains belonging to Caesar or chaotic circumstances. Instead, he said that he was bound to Christ, who was providentially in control of his life and its attendant circumstances. So, what happened to Paul and what has occurred to us in all of our varying life experiences is not without eternal significance or purpose (Rom. 8:28).

It is interesting to see how the apostle Paul's experience somewhat paralleled that of Queen Esther's. Though Esther was exiled from Judah (Esth. 2:5-10), Mordecai interpreted her presence in the court of Xerxes this way: "Who knows but that you have come to royal position for such a time as this?" (Esth. 4:14 —NIV). God's Word affirms that Esther was providentially prepared to secure deliverance for the Jews. Like Paul, Esther was not a hapless prisoner of the royal court of Xerxes. What is so incredible about her story is that the word "God" is never mentioned, and yet the imprint of his presence is clearly evident on all the pages of the book that bears her name.

As God's image bearers and children, we may find incredible security, hence serenity in the awareness that whatever occurs in our lives never happens by accident. Rather, as we submit to God's gracious will and trust him to work in us "that which is pleasing in His sight, through Jesus Christ" (Heb. 13:21 NASB), our lives will reflect a definite purpose and unquestioned significance.

❖ Insight for Foresight

"God moves in a mysterious way His wonders to perform; He plants His footsteps in the sea, and rides upon the storm. Deep in unfathomable mines of never-failing skill; He treasures up His bright designs, and *works His sovereign will*" (William Cowper).[107]

❖ Moving on from Bewilderment and Anguish to Belief and Assurance

Rick Warren observes, "You know you are maturing when you begin to see the hand of God in the random, baffling, and seemingly pointless circumstances of life"[108] (see Gen. 50:20).

❖ Leaving Our Questions and Pain in the Lord's Good Hands

Father, "I do not know, I cannot see, what God's good hand has for me, yet, this I know that overall, rules He who marks the sparrow's fall" (anonymous).[109]

Submit to God

> *Submit to God* and be at peace with him; in this way
> prosperity will come to you.
>
> Accept instruction from his mouth and lay up his
> words in your heart.
>
> If you return to the Almighty, you will be restored:
> If you remove wickedness far from your tent
>
> And assign your nuggets to the dust, your gold of
> Ophir to the rocks in the ravines,
>
> Then the Almighty will be your gold, the choicest
> silver for you.
>
> Surely then you will find delight in the Almighty
> and will lift up your face to God.
>
> —Job 22:21–26 (NIV)

Day 22—Antidote for the Sweet Poison of the False Infinite

Then the Almighty will be your gold, the choicest silver for you.
—Job 22:25 (NIV)

Many in our day seem to live only for the present, as if it held all the keys for happiness. John Eldredge writes, "So distant now from Eden, we are *desperate* for life, and we come to believe that we must arrange for it as best as we can or no one will. It is here that God must thwart us to save us from ourselves."[110] Coupled with this, Blaise Pascal said, "Thus we never live, but hope to live, and since we are always planning how to be happy, it is inevitable that we should never be so."[111]

In Mark 8:36, Jesus asked, "What shall it profit a man if he gains the entire world, but loses his own soul?" The answer is clear. There can be no benefit if one gains the world, because the meagerness of the gain is overshadowed by the immensity of the loss. Furthermore, the world is temporary, but our souls are eternal. To think that one shall find true satisfaction in anything other than God is to succumb to what Lewis calls, "The sweet poison of the false infinite."[112]

In Philippians 3, the apostle Paul explained how one might avoid succumbing to a pursuit of the false infinite. When he wrote, "What things were gain to me, those I counted loss for Christ," (Phil. 3:7 — KJV), he affirmed that knowing Christ constitutes true wealth, because such knowledge enriches the soul and has enduring value.

So, what constitutes the baseline level of satisfaction for a people wearied by the endless pursuit of satisfaction in possessions, pleasures, and projects at work? Paul, who possessed the ultimate T-shirt of T-shirts of his day (known as the Pharisee's Pharisee, and blameless as to the Pharisaical righteousness, Phil. 3:4–6), tells us in Philippians 3:8–10 that knowing Christ (the desire of nations) is the only means for experiencing total, unparalleled reality and satisfaction in this life and in the ages to come.

Paul's message then for us today is that the eternal longings of our hearts (the quest for transcendence, knowing truth, hope, meaning for life, and wholeness in our soul) are genuinely satisfied in Christ alone (note: Jn. 4:14).

Have you ever considered what an incredible step of faith it must have been for Moses to forsake all the earthly glory offered him by the Egyptian royal court? Just think that he willingly regarded "disgrace for the sake of Christ, as *greater value* than the treasures of Egypt, because he was looking ahead to his reward" (Heb. 11:26—NIV).

It is with such insightful faith and understanding that a believer in Christ today can freely pursue what really matters and endures in life, because "He that doeth the will of God abideth forever" (1 Jn. 2:17—KJV), and "They will rest from their labour, for their deeds will follow them" (Rev. 14:13—NIV).

❖ **Insight for Foresight**

Costly grace "is costly because it calls us to follow, and it is grace because when we are called to follow, the call is to follow Jesus."[113]

❖ **Moving on from Bewilderment and Anguish to Belief and Assurance**

"You really can't live without Christ. It's like, impossible to really have a really true life without him" (Cassie Bernall).[114]

❖ **Leaving Our Questions and Pain in the Lord's Good Hands**

"Lord, you are my exceeding great reward (Gen. 15:1). I thank you that there is a clear distinction between earth's temporal trinkets and heaven's enduring treasures" (1 Tim. 6:17–19).

He Will Guard the Feet of His Saints

Hannah prayed and said, "My heart rejoices in the Lord; in the Lord my horn is lifted high. My mouth boasts over my enemies for I delight in your deliverance.

"There is no one holy like the Lord; there is no one besides you; there is no Rock like our God.

"The Lord brings death and makes alive; he brings down to the grave and raises up. The Lord sends poverty and wealth; he humbles and he exalts. He raises the poor from the dust and lifts the needy from the ash heap; he seats them with princes and has them inherit a throne of honour.

"For the foundations of the earth are the Lord's; upon them he has set the world. *He will guard the feet of his saints*, but the wicked will be silenced in darkness. "It is not by strength that one prevails; those who oppose the Lord will be shattered. He will thunder against them from heaven; the Lord will judge the ends of the earth.

"He will give strength to his king and exalt the horn of his anointed."

—1 Samuel 2:1–2; 6—10 (NIV)

Day 23—Clinging to God in Spite of the Silence

Behold, I go forward but He is not there ... I cannot perceive Him.
—Job 23:8 (NASB)

Many have sought or pursued God through drugs, meditation, penitence, pilgrimages, or religious rites. The Bible directs us to understand that we may come to God by faith in Jesus Christ. When looking for Christ, we will always find Him at the cross, forgiving unworthy sinners. As he was being crucified, Jesus said to a thief on a nearby cross, "I tell you the truth, today you will be with me in paradise" (Lk. 23:43 NIV).

Though Job could not fully perceive God in the midst of his own afflictions, he nevertheless clung to him relentlessly by faith (Job 23:11-12), even when he seemed silent and remote (Job 23:8). Job's primary intent of heart was to have God vindicate his faith and confirm his integrity. He said, "I am indeed not guilty. Yet, there is no deliverance from Thy hand" (Job 10:7 NASB). Though Job 23:8 seems to raise the possibility of the inaccessibility of God ("Behold I go forward, but He is not there"), yet in verse 10 we see an overriding confidence that God is still there. Note, "*God knows* the way that I take." This confidence led Job to do the following:

❖ He recognized a meaningful purpose to his trials (Job 23:10). "I shall come forth as gold."

We may question why God places his gold in the furnace. However, when we enter a trust relationship with God, we come to see that the gold neither fears nor flees the furnace, because the refiner of the gold is there with us (Dan. 3:25; Isa. 43:2). Assured that the Lord is with us in our trials, we come to see that the painful process is not intended to distress or to destroy, but to develop and demonstrate the genuineness of our faith (1 Pet. 1:7).

❖ He retained his pursuit of God by faith in spite of trials (Job 23:11–12). "I have kept His Way."

Job followed closely to the ways of God (he held tightly to the Lord), as it was unthinkable for him to deny God in light of God's past mercies and goodness. Job allowed what he knew to be true of God in the past to inform his trust of God for the present and the future.

❖ He respected God's providential control over his trials (Job 23:13–15). "He will complete ..." (ESV).

As we attempt to grasp what is happening to us in the crucible of life's afflictions, we learn in light of Job's experience that we may have assurance that we're not hapless pawns in the toy room of a capricious deity. Indeed, there comes a time when we find relief in saying with Martin Luther, "Let God be God!" After all, He has had all eternity in which *to specialize in being God*. Yes, God knows what He is about!

❖ **Insight for Foresight**

"Of course, one must take 'sent to try us' the right way. God has not been trying an experiment on my faith or love, in order to find out their quality. He knew it already. It was I who didn't" (C. S. Lewis).[115]

❖ **Moving on from Bewilderment and Anguish to Belief and Assurance**

"When through fiery trials thy pathway shall lie, His grace all sufficient shall be thy supply; the flame shall not hurt thee, His only design, thy dross to consume, and thy gold to refine."[116]

❖ **Leaving Our Questions and Pain in the Lord's Good Hands**

"Lord, thank you that your fire does not consume us, but rather it cleanses our souls (Isa. 43:2)."

Praying the Scripture[117]

No matter what kind of Rejection you may have suffered, *Praying the Scripture* can be used By God to bring you strength.

—Beth Moore

This is my comfort in my affliction,
That Your word has revived me.

—Ps. 119:50 (NASB)

Day 24—Keep Turning the Pages

> I will visit you and fulfill my good word to
> you, to bring you back to this place.
> For I know the plans that I have for you, declares the Lord.
> —Jeremiah 29:10, 11 (NASB)

If the statement "Let your theology inform your expectations, and not your expectations your theology" ever applied, it did so during the ministry of Jeremiah, the Old Testament prophet. Sadly, the initial forecast for his nation's destiny was not bright and sunny. Instead, it was characterized by terror and foreboding. Yes, one could superimpose over the book of Jeremiah some of the famous words of Charles Dickens, who wrote, "...It was the worst of times."[118]

In fact, Jeremiah predicts a time known as "Jacob's trouble" (Jer. 30:7), thus portending one of the darkest hours in biblical history (cf. Matt. 24:21). Yet, after that distressing prophecy, the Lord graciously offsets these harbingers of sorrow and distress with promises that bring hope and encouragement to God's people.

Piercing through the dark and imminent storm clouds of Jeremiah's forecast of exile and judgment, a majestic disclosure of God's wonderful purposes for His distressed people arises. In the spirit of Jeremiah 29:11, where we read, "I know the plans I have for you, declares the Lord; plans to prosper you and not to harm you" come further, reassuring insights into God's person and purposes. Having initially confronted the nation with its sin, Jeremiah now gives reasons why believers need to cling to God by faith, by declaring in page after page a renewed vision of hope for God's people, who had received the foreboding news about impending dark days. He wrote:

- We are loved with an everlasting love (Jer. 31:3).
- God will enact a new, unconditional, binding covenant of blessing (Jer. 31:31).

- Having created heaven and earth, the almighty God can do anything (Jer. 32:17).
- In answer to our prayers, God will show us great and mighty things (Jer. 33:3).

What relief it must have brought to the heavy-hearted people of God, as the Lord led them to understand through His promises that dark times of judgment and exile would give way to the glory of restoration and blessing. The people of God will be established in their homeland, and mourning will be turned into joy (Jer. 30:17–18). Furthermore, God will enact the New Covenant and write His law on His people's hearts, thus assuring them that He will ever be their God and they would always be His people (2 Cor. 6:16–18). Are you disheartened? Let me encourage you to keep turning the pages of God's Word and celebrate the hope God's Word brings to our hearts regarding what the Lord is yet to accomplish; yes, keep looking for the morning (Ps. 30:5).

❖ Insight for Foresight

"For everything that was written in the past was written to teach us, so that through endurance and the encouragement of the Scriptures we might have hope" (Rom. 15:4 NIV).

❖ Moving on from Bewilderment and Anguish to Belief and Assurance

"That man is perfect in faith who can come to God in the utter dearth of his feelings and desires, without a glow or an aspiration, with the weight of low thoughts, failures, neglects, and wandering forgetfulness, and say to Him, 'Thou art my refuge'" (George MacDonald).[119]

❖ Leaving Our Questions and Pain in the Lord's Good Hands

Father, although "Unknown waves before me roll, hiding rock and treacherous shoal," I am glad that, "Chart and compass come from thee." Yes, "Jesus Saviour, pilot me!"[120]

Suffering According to God's Will

Dear friends, do not be surprised at the painful trial you are suffering, as though something strange were happening to you.

But rejoice that you participate in the sufferings of Christ, so that you may be overjoyed when his glory is revealed.

If you are insulted because of the name of Christ, you are blessed, for the Spirit of glory and of God rests on you.

If you suffer, it should not be as a murderer or thief or any other kind of criminal, or even as a meddler.

However, if you suffer as a Christian, do not be ashamed, but praise God that you bear that name.

So, then, those *who suffer according to God's will* should commit themselves to their faithful creator and continue to do good.

—1 Peter 4:12–16, 19 (NIV)

Day 25—Mind-Set for the Maelstrom

Oh, that I had the wings of a dove ... I would fly away and be at rest.
—Psalm 55:6 (NIV)

During a very distressing time of life, when life seemed to be driving me well beyond my resources to cope, I asked God, "Lord, please remove the pain, pressure, and pace!" Most would agree that it is quite natural to seek relief when all is in turmoil about us. We see from the above verse that the psalmist certainly did. However, the question remains: from where does relief come when we cannot "fly away"? In a word, it springs from having entrusted our burdens to God and from having embraced key truths. In Psalm 55:22, we see that one may know both relief and tranquility of heart during stressful times from which we cannot flee. The verse says, "Cast your burden upon the Lord and He will sustain you; He will never suffer the righteous to stumble." Similarly, in 1 Peter, chapter 4, believers are encouraged to bear in mind key principles, which in turn bring forth stabilizing heart-rest amidst the surging maelstrom of life's inevitable trials and stresses.

Assume That Spiritual Struggles Are Predictable for Believers—1 Peter 4:12

Do not think it strange; persecution and trials are not uncommon (cf. Jn. 15:18; 2 Tim. 3:12).

Appeal to the Privilege and Prospect That Lies Ahead—1 Peter 4:13

Philippians 1:27-29 exhorts believers to live their lives in such a way that all attacks from the harshest detractor will be refuted. The early believers counted it a joy to suffer for His name (Acts 5:41). The prospect of a future glory instills a stabilizing hope (cf. Ps. 16:11; 17:15).

Anticipate His Power—1 Peter 4:14

His glory rests (literally: "tabernacles") upon His suffering saints. Compare the grace and composure exhibited by Stephen in the face of his persecutors (Acts 6:15; 7:55–56).

Avoid the Penalty—1 Peter 4:15

Some might react adversely to trials by saying, "If this is Christianity, then give me Disneyland." Sadly, such an attitude can lead one to make some perilous future responses to trials and in the process even deprive oneself of certain key lessons in grace.

Accept Pruning Gracefully—1 Peter 4:16–18

Pruning by a skilled or prudent husbandman produces fruitfulness. Similarly, some professional photographers may develop their own film by removing it from the relative security of the camera and placing it into a pan of chemicals in a dark room, in order to achieve the desired positive results (albeit through an "uncomfortable" and "harsh" process).

Abandon Yourself to His Protection—1 Peter 4:19

"So then, those who suffer according to God's will should *commit* themselves to their faithful creator and continue to do good" (1 Pet. 4:19 NIV). The word "commit" is an accounting term, conveying the idea of depositing to the safe keeping of another, who is trustworthy.

❖ Insight for Foresight

"When God allows his people to enter the furnace, He keeps His eye on the clock and His hand on the thermostat" (Warren W. Wiersbe).[121]

❖ **Moving on from Bewilderment and Anguish to Belief and Assurance**

Psalm 4:1 (KJV) says, "Thou hast enlarged me when I was in distress." Yes, often it's in the struggle where God increases our capacity for receiving a fuller measure of his grace.

❖ **Leaving Our Questions and Pain in the Lord's Good Hands**

"Lord, when I'm too weak to fly away, help me to flee to you, my only sure refuge."

O, for a Faith That Will Not Shrink[122]
by William Bathhurst

1) *O, for a faith that will not shrink*
Though pressed by many a foe,
That will not tremble on the brink
Of any earthly woe.

2) That will not murmur nor complain
Beneath the chastening rod,
But in the hour of grief or pain
Will lean upon its God.

3) A faith that shines more bright and clear
When tempests rage without,
That, when in danger, knows no fear,
In darkness feels no doubt.

4) Lord, give me such a faith as this,
And then, whatever may come,
I'll taste even now the hallowed bliss
Of an eternal home.

Day 26—The Blessing of Staying on the Tough Road

A righteous man may have many troubles, but
the Lord delivers him from them all.

—Psalm 34:19 (NIV)

The Late Ruth Bell Graham wrote, "We have an umbrella tree in our living room. Because it is not native to where we live, it makes a nice houseplant, growing to 10 feet tall at most. But in a tropical climate it can grow to 40 feet. Why should we wonder, then, when we Christians struggle? We are not native plants. The earth is not our home, and we can expect to have rough times. Our Lord promised us that. But we also have this promise: 'Blessed is the man who perseveres under trial, because when he has stood the test, he will receive the crown of life that God has promised to those who love him'" (Jam. 1:12 NIV).[123]

In 1996, I was privileged to attend the oral defense of a doctoral dissertation presented by Romanian pastor Joseph Thon at the American College of Louvain, Belgium. Pastor Thon, who had suffered much under the Ceausescu regime, cited the importance of the Doctrine of Suffering for the life of a believer, and how believers might stand up under suffering and persevere. The following points summarize his dissertation:[124]

1. Believers who have suffered for faithfulness to the Gospel will be rewarded (2 Tim. 4:6–8).
2. Suffering for righteousness draws us nearer to Christ. Paul wrote, "That I may know Him and the fellowship of His suffering" (Phil. 3:10).
3. Suffering purges Christians from self-reliance, lest they become proud (2 Cor. 1:8–10 and 2 Cor. 12:7,9; and Isa. 38:15–17).

4. Suffering within the will of God silences the false accusations of Satan, in that the authenticity of a believer's faith is confirmed in accepting it patiently (1 Pet. 4:14-16).
5. Suffering provides a catalyst for the growth of the church. In the book of Acts 5:40–42, we see how persecution often resulted in further effective proclamation of the Gospel.

When Satan or the world seeks to silence believers through hardship, scripture reminds us that we may overcome by faith. In 1 John 5: 4b, it says, "This is the victory that has overcome the world, even our faith." In Revelation 12:7-8, 11, and 14 (respectively), we read other encouraging truths in this regard:

- The dragon was not strong enough to defeat the angel Michael.
- The saints of God overcame the evil one by the blood of the Lamb and their testimony.
- The Woman (Israel) will be cared for during her escape to the wilderness.

❖ **Insight for Foresight**

"My comfort in my suffering is this: Your promise preserves my life" (Ps. 119:50 NIV).

❖ **Moving on from Bewilderment and Anguish to Belief and Assurance**

"But what of those of us who stay with the tough road we are on? How do we survive, live our lives to the fullness of what is on offer? I have found that in everything that happens to me there is a path of hope and faith, which constantly surprises. In the darkest times, there is light and that light banishes the darkness; in fact, the darkness flees from this light. In times of need, something always happens to ensure we find that all our needs are satisfied" (E. Cross).[125]

❖ Leaving Our Questions and Pain in the Lord's Good Hands

"Lord, thank you for the truth, 'Greater is He who is in you, than he who is in the world' (1 Jn. 4:4). Therefore, I gladly hide myself beneath the shadow of your wings for refuge from the enemy of my soul, 'Whom the God of peace shall soon crush under your feet'" (Rom. 16:20).

The Hand That Holds

The hand that holds the ocean's depths
Can hold my small affairs;
The hand that guides the universe
Can carry all my cares.

—Author Unknown

CHRIS GOPPERT

Day 27—Parking Our Minds

> Though the fig tree should not blossom … and the fields produce
> no food … I will exult in the Lord, I will rejoice in the God
> of my salvation … He has made my feet like hind's feet.
> —Habakkuk 3:17–19 (NASB)

I once owned a Porsche (stripped down, basic model but for real). Sometimes I wonder if it did not actually own me. My friend Hank also owned a Porsche (more expensive and not so basic). He parked it on the street one night. Sadly, a drunk driver came around the corner that same night. His vehicle collided with Hank's Porsche, crushing the engineering marvel and in the process stripping the gears. It was an expensive mistake to not park it in a garage. The upshot of this true story is that it does matter where we park our car. If it is parked in the wrong place, it may spell the difference between driving or walking (not to mention the potential for economic woes!).

Shifting the emphasis to a spiritual application for our lives, one soon comes to appreciate that where we park our *minds* is far more critical and can spell the difference between faith or faltering, panic or peace, and apprehensiveness or assurance. Parking our mental car under the shadow of flights of fancy, alcoholic binges, shopping sprees, affairs, or simply bailing out of reality is nearly always a bad choice, with worse consequences. However, parking our mental car in the garage of truth will spare us from confusion, chaos, and collapse.

Habakkuk, an Old Testament prophet, knew where to park his mind. His example of how to think in a time of great distress helps guide our own responses in hard times. In Habakkuk 3:17–19, we see that even though an impending calamity threatened to strip the land of crops, create chills in the pit of his stomach, or consternation in his heart, Habakkuk was nevertheless confident (v. 18), because God was his strength (v. 19). Being confident in God's glory filling the earth (2:14),

His control over all circumstances, and the promise of His awesome deliverance,

Habakkuk was enabled to derive spiritual strength to go on to, or climb the heights, and to know stability of heart in a difficult personal and national crisis. Of interest, Habakkuk means *He Who Clings*. Point: He who clings, climbs!

If we think that celebrated athletes, catwalk models, CEOs, and movie stars always have the easiest of lives, all the fun, and that they are the truly significant people in this world, then we are parking our minds in the wrong place. If we conclude that what we do will never amount to anything and that no one will ever notice or care about what we think or represent, we do ourselves a serious injustice, because it is simply not true. It is pure fantasy and not reality to think that the rich and famous of this world are the only significant or happy people. We must be careful to see ourselves as God sees us (created in His image and rich in faith [James 2:5]) and then process our perceptions of reality through the framework of biblical truth, which enables us to think on whatever things are "true, honourable, right and pure" (Phil. 4:8 NASB). Yes, parking our minds in the right place is indispensable for attaining a clarifying perspective and the continuous peace of God in unsettling and uncertain times.

❖ Insight for Foresight

"You do not live in a mechanistic world ruled by necessity; you don't live in a random world ruled by chance; you live in a world ruled by the God of Exodus and Easter" (E. H. Peterson).[126]

❖ Moving on from Bewilderment and Anguish to Belief and Assurance

Habakkuk said that God had made his feet to be like hind's feet. "As the hind's front feet mark the steps in which their rear feet follow, so God marks out the steps of His will before us. Our part is to place our feet in His steps."[127]

❖ **Leaving Our Questions and Pain in the Lord's Good Hands**

Father, may I so immerse my soul in the depths of your truth that its counsel and comfort will well up in my heart to overflowing praise and peace.

Blessings out of Pain[128]

It is a part of God's great plan to adapt His mercies to the woes of mankind. Often calamity, poverty and sickness are permitted so that He may show the provisions of His mercy, that He may teach us to prize His blessings, and that deep-felt gratitude may bind us to Him.

—Albert Barnes

You made men ride over our heads;
We went through fire and water,
Yet you brought us out into a place
of abundance.

—Ps. 66:12 (NASB)

Day 28—When Talking to Oneself Makes Sense

> Why are you in despair, O my Soul? And why have you become
> disturbed within me? Hope in God, for I shall again praise
> Him for the help of His presence. —Psalm 42:5–6 (NASB)

Have you ever felt your emotions soaring one moment, seemingly far above the clouds, only to have them cascade down into a whirlpool of dismay the next? It would be a rare person indeed who never asked, why am I so disheartened? Why do I feel down or blue, for no apparent reason? Why do I stagger about like a dazed prizefighter caught unaware by a sudden, unexpected uppercut to the chin?

By way of application, are the provocative taunting and maddening ravings of the godless so powerful that they can override the awareness of God's kindness for His children (see Nehemiah 4:1–15)? All of these are good questions and are not uncommon responses to the universal experience of managing one's emotions in seasons of heaviness of heart.

As with other lament psalms, Psalm 42 allows us to hear the heart's cry of a person wearied by emotional despondency, arising in particular from the reproach of his enemies (v. 10) and his desire to renew intimate fellowship with God and His people (vv. 1–4). Such conditions can only truly be remedied by the renewal, uplifting, and refreshment that God by the presence of His Spirit can bring to a heavy heart. The intensity of the writer's longing for the keen sense of God's presence is dramatically underscored by the words, "Tears have been my food," (v. 3) and, "Now I am deeply discouraged" (v. 6)!

In particular, Psalm 42 shows us that God understands that weariness of heart can result from the provocations and slander of the godless. To minister to this particular point of our need, God in faithfulness directs his love toward us daily and at night, when our minds are active with countless conflicting thoughts (Ps. 94:17–19). His song remains with us (Ps. 42:8).

From the psalmist's perspective, the prospect for renewed hope ("*For I shall yet praise Him, my savior and my God*," v. 5) and relief from dismay was not a pipe dream. By way of encouragement for ourselves, the imminent prospect for renewal is not founded on wishful thinking but on the reality of our having had sufficient personal experiences in the past with many excursions into God's gracious blessings and ways (v. 4). So, what does this mean? We may, with confidence, most assuredly anticipate a lifting up of our downcast spirits. Yes, we may hope again! Knowing that God is our rock and helper (vv. 9, 11) our soul is stirred to renewed praise.

❖ **Insight for Foresight**

"When the writer of this psalm said, 'So pants my soul after thee, O God' (Ps. 42:1 KJV), it was neither ease, nor honor that he sought, but the enjoyment of communion with God as the most urgent need of his soul. Such a relationship with God Himself was viewed not merely as the sweetest of luxuries, but as an absolute necessity."[129]

❖ **Moving on from Bewilderment and Anguish to Belief and Assurance**

"Be still, my soul—thy God doth undertake to guide the future as He has the past; Thy hope, thy confidence let nothing shake—All now mysterious shall be bright at last. Be still, my soul—the waves and winds still know His voice, who ruled them while He dwelt below."[130]

❖ **Leaving Our Questions and Pain in the Lord's Good Hands**

"O safe to the Rock that is higher than I, my soul in its conflicts and sorrows would fly; so sinful, so weary—Thine would I be: Thou blest 'Rock of Ages,' I'm hiding in Thee."[131]

Our Eyes Are Upon Thee!

And Jehoshaphat was afraid and turned his attention to seek the Lord; and proclaimed a fast throughout all Judah. So, Judah gathered together to seek help from the Lord; they even came from all the cities of Judah to seek the Lord.

Then Jehoshaphat stood in the assembly of Judah and Jerusalem, in the house of the Lord before the new court, and he said, "O Lord, the God of our fathers, art Thou not God in the heavens? And art Thou not ruler over all the kingdoms of the nations? Power and might are in Thy hand so that no one can stand against Thee. "Didst Thou not, O our God, drive out the inhabitants of this land before Thy people Israel, and give it to the descendants of Abraham Thy friend forever? And they lived in it, and have built Thee a sanctuary there for Thy name, saying,

'Should evil come upon us, the sword, or judgment, or pestilence, or famine, we will stand before this house and before Thee (for Thy name is in this house) and cry to Thee in our distress, and Thou wilt hear and deliver us.'

"And now behold, the sons of Ammon and Moab and Mount Seir, whom Thou didst not let Israel invade when they came out of the land of Egypt (they turned aside from them and did not destroy them),

"Behold how they are rewarding us, by coming to drive us out from Thy possession which Thou hast given us as an inheritance. O our God, wilt Thou not judge them? For we are powerless before this great multitude who are coming against us; nor do we know what to do, *but our eyes are on Thee.*"

—2 Chronicles 20:3–12 (KJV)

Day 29—When the Dreaded Becomes Embedded

> O our God…we are powerless before this great
> multitude who are coming against us; nor do we
> know what to do, but our eyes are on you.
> —2 Chronicles 20:12 (NASB)

Would it surprise you that a good Judean king, whose heart was fully devoted to God, experienced what he had dreaded (Job 3:25) and confessed that he did not know what to do when hearing bad news? In 2 Chronicles 20, we see how Jehoshaphat responded when the dreaded became embedded!

- **His Position**: vs. 1–2, **A Report**: "Enemies in the Land!" News regarding an imminent enemy invasion reaches the ears of the king, and he becomes alarmed. He has just finished one battle, (2 Chron. 18:28–34), and now he is being threatened again. This portion of God's Word reminds us of the enemy of our souls who, like an enraged lion (1 Pet. 5:7–8), prowls about, waiting to attack yet again (Lk. 4:13).
- **His Posture**: vs. 3–4, **Resolve**: "To inquire of the Lord." In his alarm, there is control! The king was resolved to seek God and not military intervention. He did not panic but instead, he sought God's help, knowing God's commitment to His people's welfare. At a crucial time, the king leads Judah by decisive example and action.
- **His Prayer**: vs. 5–12, **Realization**: "You rule over all." Jehoshaphat's prayer was not a random stab toward heaven, but was part of a cultivated practice of seeking God in all seasons of life (2 Chron. 18:31). By confessing that God rules over all, he confirmed his trust in God.
- **His Perspective**: vs. 10–12, **Realistic**: "But Now" and "No Power!" Jehoshaphat identifies the problem confronting the people. He says, "But now, here are men determined to do us harm," and, "Look, we have no power!" In effect, "This is beyond my reserve but not God's resources!"

- **His Persuasion**: v. 12, **Rely**! "Our eyes are upon you!" This is another way of saying we are not relying on our wisdom, plans, or experience to find a way out of this dilemma (Prov. 3:5). The people stood expectantly, and God responded. Note David's confidence in Psalm 62:5, "My expectation is from the Lord" (KJV)!
- **His Pronouncement**: v. 20, **Reassurance**: "You will be upheld!" The expectation for deliverance is linked directly to the exhortation to heed the prophets and God's Word. The king's stirring exhortation, "Have faith in the Lord your God and you will be upheld; have faith in His prophets and you will be successful" (2 Chron. 20:20), inspired the people to move forward in the belief they would experience God's victory over their enemies (2 Chron. 20:15, 17).

❖ **Insight for Foresight**

"I have no doubt that Providence guided us, across the storm-white sea that separated Elephant Island from our landing-place on South Georgia. I know that during that long march over the unnamed mountains and glaciers … it seemed to me often that we were four, not three."[132]

❖ **Moving on from Bewilderment and Anguish to Belief and Assurance**

Do we see panic or peace in the way Jehoshaphat approaches his problem? How significant was the king's practice of prayer and pondering the scriptures for developing within his heart the cultivated response of calling on the Lord at such a key time as this (cf. 2 Chron. 18:31)?

❖ **Leaving Our Questions and Pain in the Lord's Good Hands**

"O bring your praise to God above, the fountain of eternal love, whose mercy firm through ages past has stood and shall forever last" (author unknown).

Moment by Moment[133]

There are very few school children who have not heard at some point, that all roads seemingly lead to Rome. Well, it does not take long for the believer to learn by experience that all moments in life are opportune occasions to focus on God.

Rick Warren notes,

In Happy Moments, Praise God!

In Difficult Moments, Seek God!

In Quiet Moments, Worship God!

In Painful Moments, Trust God!

In Every Moment, Thank God!

Praise the Lord!
For it is good to sing praises to our God;
For it is pleasant and praise
Is becoming.

—Ps. 147:1 (NASB)

Day 30—Deciphering the Design of a Divine Delay

Lord...if you had been here, my brother would not have died.
—John 11:21 (NIV)

Soon after Lazarus, a friend of Jesus, passes away, Jesus arrives in Lazarus's village, Bethany. Upon his arrival, Jesus Immediately seizes the moment to address the lingering questions occupying Mary and Martha's hearts regarding God's purposes for the death, by speaking to the issue that doubtless perplexed them, namely: Why would Jesus delay His arrival, and could there be another purpose transcending the need of healing that they could not discern? Initially, it seems strange that Jesus did not come earlier to bring healing to His friend Lazarus, whom he loved, but then God has his good reasons.

Now, to appreciate better the Lord's purpose in allowing his friend Lazarus to die, we see in verse 6 that Jesus (aware of the impending death) chose to delay His trip. In verses 11 and 15, we see why. Not only was Jesus going to Bethany to awaken Lazarus, but equally importantly, He would awaken within His disciples' hearts a vital awareness of who He was and show them that the incredible power that would raise Lazarus was now available to those who believe (Eph. 1:18–20). Yes, the Lord knows that if we are to trust Him more, we need to know Him better. As we come to verse 25, Martha and Mary see clearly that Jesus is, at all times, the living Savior and vital resurrection life itself, which they might not have known had Jesus not met them in the valley of the shadow of death. This story reminds us that there are times when we will be disappointed, because our expectations may be unrealistic or self-centered. However, Martha and Mary illustrate well how we may handle the tension between groaning in grief and growing in grace when waiting for God to intervene. What is striking about Martha and Mary's laments is the confidence overriding their initial disappointment: "Lord, had you been here, Lazarus would not have died" (Jn. 11:21, 32).

So, when we cannot discern a divine purpose behind the seemingly interminable delay by God to respond to our heart's cry (to save a loved one from dying), we may find ourselves tottering between resolve of heart and resignation of spirit. Yes, in spite of all we believe, we may, on occasion, find ourselves faltering in the face of trials. So, why is that? Charles Swindoll has a helpful contemplative word of grace. "Of all the doubts which, as Robert Browning writes, 'rap and knock and enter in our soul,' perhaps few are more devastating than those that happen when we are told by God in effect, 'Wait, wait, wait, wait, wait, wait!' And we wrestle deeply with His timing."[134]

Understandably, the process by which we learn to accept God's timing is never easy, but afterwards, thankfully, we may rejoice as the process develops our character (Rom. 5:3–5). Perhaps we can learn a helpful insight about how to exercise implicit trust during those extended waiting periods by observing Mary's act of abiding trust (see how she casts herself before Jesus in reverence, clinging to Him in her brokenness, v. 32). Such a posture of heart will keep us from the tendency to cry "foul" or "victim" and thereby persevere in unwavering trust in God's integrity of heart.

❖ Insight for Foresight

"Prayer is request. The essence of request, as distinct from compulsion, is that it may or may not be granted. And if an infinitely wise Being listens to the requests of finite and foolish creatures, of course He will sometimes grant and sometimes refuse them."[135]

❖ Moving on from Bewilderment and Anguish to Belief and Assurance

"It is a great matter when in extreme need to take hold of prayer. I know that, whenever I earnestly prayed, I have been amply heard and have obtained more than I prayed for. God sometimes delayed, but at last He came."[136]

❖ Leaving Our Questions and Pain in the Lord's Good Hands

"Lord Jesus, we do not seek you in prayer because we believe prayer works, but rather we believe in the reality of your presence and power, and therefore we pray in faith believing (Mark 11:24)!"

Exclude the Possibility of Suffering?[137]

Many are the afflictions of the righteous,
but the Lord delivers him out of them all.
—Ps. 34:19 (NASB)

There can be little doubt as to the universal testimony of Scripture, that suffering and hardship are inescapable facts of life.

C.S. Lewis stated,

Try to exclude the possibility of suffering which the order of nature and the existence of free will involve, and you will find that you have excluded life itself.

These things I have spoken to you, so that in Me you may have peace. In the world you have tribulation, but take courage; I have overcome the world.

—John 16:33 (NASB)

Day 31—Stones of Remembrance

> Samuel took a stone and set it up … He named it
> Ebenezer, saying, "Thus far has the Lord helped us."
> —1 Samuel 7:12 (NIV)

Over the last thirty-five years, I have collected stones from various parts of the world (Ireland, Israel, South Africa, and Zimbabwe). Occasionally, as I glance at these stones, I am reminded of many significant memories associated with each place we have visited or where we have lived.

As a means of encouraging believers to recall God's faithfulness and to anticipate His continued involvement in their lives, the Lord gave instructions to Israel to erect pillars of stones as memorials or reminders of God's care (Josh. 4:1–7). In our day and age, we do not erect literal stone memorials celebrating all that God has done, but we can set apart in our hearts "stones of remembrance." These "stones" remind us of God's personal involvement in and gracious oversight of our spiritual journey.

At a particularly distressing time in his life, the psalmist Asaph wondered if the Lord had forsaken Him. He asked, "Will the Lord reject forever? Will he never show his favor again? Has his unfailing love vanished forever? Has his promise failed for all time? Has God forgotten to be merciful? Has he in anger withheld his compassion?" (Ps. 77:7–9). Then, by reflecting on how God had worked in his life, Asaph was able to move beyond his questions to specific assurances, based on the presence of certain key memorial stones he had erected in the past. He wrote: "Then I thought: To this *I will appeal:* the years of the right hand of the Most-High. I will *remember* the deeds of the Lord; yes, I will remember your miracles of long ago. I will *meditate* on all your works and *consider* all your mighty deeds" (Ps. 77:10–12 NIV).

What helps to highlight the authentic flavor of the Psalms is the transparency of believers such as Asaph, who in the midst of struggles and questions, learned the importance of appropriating heart-rest through an implicit trust in the immensity of God's gracious sovereignty. Asaph shares this insight. He wrote, "My flesh and my heart may fail ... but as for me, it is good to be near God; *I have made* the sovereign Lord my refuge" (Ps. 73:26, 28 NIV). Think of it, God, most high, who inhabits eternity, who indwells the most contrite and humble of hearts, not only desires to be our secure refuge, but also, He has committed Himself to protect us from the crippling effects of disillusionment and unbelief. Note in Psalm 73:28 the writer freely chose, he was not forced to make God his refuge, and he felt safe in God's presence (he was not threatened by such an awesome relationship).

Stones of remembrance are designed to serve as memorials to God's special working in the lives of His children. Psalm 111:4 (NIV), says, "He has caused his wonders to be remembered ..." Yes, stones that we have piled up high are difficult to ignore or forget. By consciously recording the accounts of God's goodness and faithfulness to us in a prominent place, such as a journal, we will have the means of setting up lasting memorials that will remind us of God's care, serving to nurture our faith and bolster our hope. From such memorials, we may draw enduring strength of heart that will enable us to persevere in our trust in God.

❖ **Insight for Foresight**

"Trusting in the sovereignty of God can turn outrage into compassion; hatred into concern."[138]

❖ **Moving on from Bewilderment and Anguish to Belief and Assurance**

"For the Mighty One has done great things for me; And holy is His name" (Lk. 1:49 NASB).[139]

❖ **Leaving Our Questions and Pain in the Lord's Good Hands**

"Thank you, Lord, that I can now look back on my life and see not just devastation with bits and parts strewn here and there along the pathway, but rather, I see stones set up, one upon another, signifying that you are working to build a lasting monument of your incredible grace in Christ."

> They will enter Zion with singing; Everlasting joy will
> crown their heads. Gladness and joy will overtake
> them, And sorrow and *sighing will flee away.*
> —Isaiah 35:10 (NIV)

Part III

A Primer on Suffering

The days of the blameless are known to the Lord …
in times of disaster they will not wither.
—Psalm 37:18–19 (NIV)

The Wider Context of Our Brokenness[140]

So often, the words 'devastated' and 'broken' bleed through into the conversation, when hurting people share the account of their walk with pain. Colson develops this observation further when he adds a redemptive note.

As fallen creatures we are metaphorically full of broken bones ... when God resets the broken bones of our character, it hurts.

Much of the sting is taken out of the brokenness ... if we can see it within some wider context of purpose. God's purposes ... give meaning and significance ...to suffering.

—Charles Colson

For which cause we faint not; but though our outward man perish, yet the inward man is renewed day by day.
—2 Cor. 4:16

A Primer on Suffering

A theological framework for helping us to better understand
the place for suffering within the will of God.

But those who suffer he delivers in their suffering;
He speaks to them In their affliction.
—Job 36:15 (NIV)

Cherish Your Scars[141]

At times the scars and hurts we bear can appear to be pointless. Author Bodie Thoene encourages us to transform that pain we feel into meaningful worship and anticipation of a glorious future day when grief will be cast off for eternal gladness of spirit.

Cherish your scars ... They make you more like Him.
Proof you've fought the battle here below.
Christ crucified, the only begotten Son of God sacrificed for you.

And at the foot of the cross, most human of all agony, Grieve like Mary at the grave for all you cannot understand.

Give up to God the hopes your love has begotten.
Mourn at the tomb of what you've lost.

Then give up to God what you cannot change.
Remember there will be Easter morning; Resurrection!
—Bodie Thoene

Finally, let no one cause me trouble, For I bear on my body the marks of Jesus.

—Gal. 6:17 (NIV)

A Primer on Suffering

The Essential Character of God and the Question of Suffering

Wendell Phelps lectured in English for forty-one years at Yale University. At the end of one winter term, he was marking a particular exam paper when he noted that with the exception of a singular comment by the student, the exam paper was blank. The comment read, "Only God knows the answer to this question; Merry Christmas." Professor Phelps responded, "God gets an A, you fail; Happy New Year."[142]

For countless centuries, detractors of the Christian faith have confronted believers with a seemingly impossible question to answer and an imponderable dilemma to come to terms with, namely, how can God expect people to trust Him when He:

- allows evil to exist;
- permits good people to be afflicted with hardship and suffering; and
- receives ultimate glory after suffering refines the sufferer?

Several years ago, a popular book appeared, written by a religious teacher, that attempted to address the perennially nagging theological and philosophical question (theodicy) of why a good God can allow evil to exist in His creation and even serve His purpose of refining the faith of believers. According to various reviewers, such as Dr. Norman Geisler, the overall premise of the book was that the author essentially traded in on his view of an all-powerful God for just a good God, thus inferring that God allows sickness and suffering because He cannot stop it from happening. For further study, readers may wish to refer to the book title indicated in endnote.[143]

If, on the one hand, the contention of the author referred to above, regarding why bad things happen to so-called good people, offers a momentary, albeit minimal assuagement to a pressing intellectual inquiry of the larger philosophic question on suffering, then on the other hand, its inability to comfort the afflicted with a more positive hope results in a woefully inadequate treatise.

In essence, the conclusion fails to provide the means for granting any sustainable comfort for those who suffer, or assurance that they are not at the mercy of evil, or impersonal capricious fates, or the unpredictable whim of natural forces.

Given the reality of such a realistic dilemma, one may rightfully appeal for a frame of reference that allows one to believe that there is a sovereign and personal God who is in control of life, while permitting the vagaries of free choice in fallen humankind and the presence of disease and death to coexist.

In seeking to know how to reconcile God's goodness with the presence of evil in this world, Hannah Whithall-Smith wrote:

> "Nothing else matters as much as this, for all our salvation depends wholly and entirely upon what God is; if He cannot be proved to be absolutely good, and absolutely unselfish, then our case is hopeless."[144]

The Lord Will Rescue Me

Alexander the metalworker did me a *great deal of harm*. The Lord will repay him for what he has done.

You too should be on your guard against him, because *he strongly* opposed our message.

At my first defense, no one came to my support, but *everyone deserted* me. May it not be held against them.

But the Lord stood at my side and gave me strength, so that through me the message might be fully proclaimed and all the Gentiles might hear it. And I was delivered from the lion's mouth.

The Lord will rescue me from every evil attack and will bring me safely to his heavenly kingdom. To him be glory forever and ever. Amen.

—2 Timothy 4:14–18 (NIV)

Though some have suggested that God is not good if He allows suffering, and that suffering cannot of necessity be a good thing, scripture affirms categorically that God is entirely good all the time and that suffering can be beneficial to those whose trust is in Him (Rom. 8:28). The following short story may help to illustrate this truth.

A Christian woman had fallen and broken her leg. After being attended to by a doctor, she had a visit from her pastor, (Lloyd Ogilvie, of Hollywood Presbyterian Church). She said to him, "I see no reason for this happening to me … I cannot *see* how any good can come from it!" After a few moments, he gently said to her, "Our Bible does not say, 'We *see* that all things work for good,' but rather, 'We *know* that in all things, God works for the good of those who love Him, and are called according to His purposes.'"

Perhaps the tension arising from a good God allowing evil to exist and to serve his purposes can partially be resolved if we look beyond the common view of "good" (pleasant, comfortable, right, free from pain) and see "good" as that which enriches humankind and glorifies God. Perhaps only then can we begin to appreciate the depth of God's wisdom in matters we cannot fathom (Deut. 29:29; Rom. 11:33–36).

In *The Problem of Pain*, C. S. Lewis wrote:

> The problem of reconciling human suffering with the existence of a God, who loves is only insoluble so long as we attach a trivial meaning to the word 'love', and look on things as if man were the centre of them. Man is not the centre. God does not exist for the sake of man. Man does not exist for his own sake, "Thou has created all things, and for Thy pleasure they are and were created" (Rev. 4:11 KJV).

We were made not primarily that we may love God (though we were made for that too), but that God may love us, that we may become objects in which the divine love may rest "well-pleased."[145]

As simplistic as it may initially appear, it is nevertheless heartening to realize that when we cannot discern any conclusive or perfect answers to why suffering is a reality in our lives, it is helpful to know that our experience with pain is not that different from what other friends have encountered and that, best of all, there are enduring assurances that inform our faith and fortify our soul in such times.

With that above thought in mind, the reader will find the following pages to be useful, as they reflect in part many of those enduring assurances and principles that lend clarifying perspectives on the place of suffering and affliction in our lives.

Some Time We'll Understand[146]

by James McGranahan

Not now, but in the coming years,
It may be in the better land,
We'll read the meaning of our tears,
And there, some time, we'll understand.

Chorus:

> Then trust in God through all the days; Fear not, for He does hold
> thy hand; Though dark thy way, still sing and praise,
> Some time, some time, we'll understand.

We'll catch the broken thread again, And finish what we here began;
Heaven will the mysteries explain, And then, ah, then, we'll understand.

Chorus

We'll know why clouds instead of sun
Were over many a cherished plan;
Why song has ceased when scarce begun;
It is there, some time, we'll understand.

Chorus

God knows the way, He holds the key,
He guides with unerring hand;
Some time with fearless eyes we'll see;
Yes, there, up there, we'll understand.

Chorus

General Observations on the Topic of Suffering

A United States Census Bureau statistic indicates that fifty-one million people (18 percent of the population of the United States) have some level of disability, and 32 million (12 percent) have a severe disability. Amongst Americans age eighty and older, 72 percent are disabled. According to one US Government Census finding, the odds are that we, or someone in our family will be affected by the challenges disability brings. Disability is clearly not the only form of suffering, but it is, nevertheless, a significant reality confronting a huge number of people, including those closest to us.[147]

For centuries, the painful reality of suffering has attracted universal attention of notable sages and scholars alike. It is without question a sobering fact that has characterized much of life and has found a voice in our literature. Even J.R.R. Tolkien's beloved hobbits Merry and Pippin (*The Two Towers*) found that life beyond the relative security of their beloved shire was cruel and threatening.

Having been taken captive by their enemies, they found themselves comparing notes and "talking lightly in hobbit fashion of the things that had happened since their capture. No listener would have guessed from their words that they had suffered cruelly, and been in dire peril going without hope towards torment and death; or that even now, as they knew well, they had little chance of ever finding friend or safety again."[148]

Human suffering may take many different forms, such as:

o   being worn down by strong temptations that weigh heavily on us
o   standing alone as a pillar of righteousness in a secular workplace
o   agonizing over the spiritual condition of one who is not following the Lord
o   hearing a heartless remark uttered about a special-needs child

o feeling rejection or facing ostracism after witnessing (reproach of the cross)
o enduring a painfully chronic, physical malady
o bearing scars from traumatic physical or mental torture
o undergoing deep and unresolved emotional grief over the loss of a loved one, in particular, owing to tragic circumstances
o bearing hurts from sadistic and abusive parents or spouse
o losing one's home, pension, and once-secure source of employment
o undergoing verbal or physical attack without cause (Ps. 27:12; 59:4; and 119:161)
o being discriminated against because of gender, ethnicity, religion or political affiliation.

But the God of all grace, who hath called us unto His eternal
glory by Christ Jesus, after that ye have suffered a while,
make you perfect, stablish, strengthen, settle you.
—1 Peter 5:10 (KJV)

He Is Able to Help

For surely it is not angels he helps, But, Abraham's descendants.
For this reason, he had to be made like his brothers in every way,
In order that he might become a merciful and faithful high priest
in service to God,
And that he might make atonement for the sins of the people.
Because he himself *suffered* when he was tempted, *He is able to help*
those who are being tempted.

—Hebrews 2:16–18 (NIV)

The Bible's Realistic View of Suffering

Upon a fair and objective reading of the entire Bible, one will see that the Bible is not dismissive of one's suffering and its consequent distress upon the soul. The following examples are but a sampling of many appropriate texts available throughout the Bible.

"A righteous man may have many troubles, but the Lord delivers him from them all …" (Ps. 34:19 NIV).

"Each day has enough trouble of its own" (Mt. 6:34 NIV).

"If they persecuted me, they will persecute you also" (Jn. 15:20 NIV).

"You, however, know all about my teaching, my way of life, my purpose, faith, patience, love and endurance, the persecutions I endured. Yet the Lord rescued me from all of them" (2 Tim. 3:10-11 NIV).

"Consider it pure joy, my brothers, whenever you face trials of many kinds …" (Jam. 1:2 NIV).

"But if you suffer for doing good and you endure it, this is commendable before God … to this you were called, because Christ suffered for you, leaving you an example, that you should follow in His steps" (1 Pet. 2:20–21 NIV).

"It is better, if it is God's will, to suffer for doing good, than for doing evil" (1 Pet. 3:17 NIV).

"Dear friends, do not be surprised at the painful trial you are suffering, as though something strange were happening to you" (1 Pet. 4:12 NIV).

Self-denial destroys the very root and foundation of sorrow.[149]
—Jonathan Edwards, 1723

Tell It to Jesus[150]

by E.S. Lorenz and J.E. Rankin

Are you weary, are you heavy-hearted? Tell it to Jesus, Tell it to Jesus;
Are you grieving over joys departed? Tell it to Jesus alone.

Chorus:

> Tell it to Jesus, tell it to Jesus,
> He is a friend that's well known;
> You've no other—such a friend or brother,
> Tell it to Jesus alone.

Do the tears flow down your cheeks unbidden? Tell it to Jesus, Tell it to Jesus;
Have you sins that to men's eyes are hidden? Tell it to Jesus alone.

Chorus

Do you fear the gathering clouds of sorrow? Tell it to Jesus, Tell it to Jesus;
Are you anxious what shall be tomorrow? Tell it to Jesus alone.

Chorus

Are you troubled at the thought of dying? Tell it to Jesus,
Tell it to Jesus; For Christ's coming Kingdom are you sighing?
Tell it to Jesus alone.

Chorus

The Bible Offers Specific Reasons for Our Afflictions

"You intended to harm me, but God intended it for good to accomplish what is now being done, the saving of many lives" (Gen. 50:20 NIV).

"He humbled you ... to teach you ..." (Deut. 8:3 NIV).

"For you, O, God, tested us; you brought us into prison and laid burdens on our backs ... we went through fire and water, but you brought us to a place of abundance" (Ps. 66:10–12 NIV).

"If we are distressed, it is for your comfort and salvation" (2 Cor. 1:6 NIV).

"You may have had to suffer grief in all kinds of trials. These have come so that your faith—of greater worth than gold, which perishes, even though refined by fire—may be proved genuine" (1 Pet. 1:6–7 NIV).

"It is good for me that I was afflicted, that I might learn your statutes" (Ps. 119:71).

The reader may also appreciate reading Malcolm Muggeridge's *A Twentieth Century Testimony*, where he assesses amongst many things, the benefits of affliction in his life.[151]

The Bible Directs Our Hearts to a Place of Sure Refuge When We Suffer

"Let the beloved of the Lord rest secure in him, for he shields him all day long, and the one the Lord loves rests between his shoulders" (Deut. 33:12 NIV).

"God is our refuge and strength; an ever-present help in trouble" (Ps. 46:1 NIV).

"He will cover you with his feathers, and under his wings you will find refuge; his faithfulness will be your shield, and rampart. You will not fear the terror of night, nor the arrow that flies by day" (Ps. 91:4–5 NIV).

"You have been a refuge ... for the needy in his distress" (Isa. 25:4 NIV).

"But when he (Peter) saw the wind, he was afraid and, *beginning* to sink, cried out, 'Lord, save me!' Immediately Jesus reached out his hand and caught him" (Matt. 14:30–31 NIV).

"I have told you these things, so that in me you may have peace. In this world, you will have trouble. But take heart! I have overcome the world" (Jn. 16:33 NIV).

"The Lord also will be a refuge for the oppressed, a refuge in times of trouble, and they that know thy name will put their trust in thee; For thou, Lord, hast not forsaken those who seek thee" —Ps. 9:9-10 (KJV).

From Every Stormy Wind[152]

From every stormy wind that blows, From every swelling
tide of woes, There is a calm; a sure retreat:
It is found beneath the mercy seat.

There is a place where Jesus sheds
The oil of gladness on our heads;
A place than all besides, more-sweet:
It is the blood bought mercy seat.

There is a scene where spirits blend, Where friend holds
fellowship with friend; Though sundered far, by faith
they meet Around one common mercy seat.

Ah! Whither could we flee for aid, When tempted,
desolate, dismayed; Or how the hosts of hell defeat,
Had suffering saints no mercy seat?
—Hugh Stowell

Is Suffering Directly Related to Personal or Collective Sin?

In the New Testament Gospel of Luke, chapter 13, we find that the Lord Jesus not only welcomes our interaction on life's tough questions and hard issues, but He Himself takes the initiative to ask, in turn, pointed questions with respect to the matter of whether suffering is always directly related to our having sinned or not. In this helpful passage of scripture, Jesus brings refreshing clarity to this perennially-nagging question.

"Jesus answered, 'Do you think that these Galileans were worse sinners than all the other Galileans because they suffered this way? I tell you, no! But unless you repent, you too will all perish'" (Lk. 13:1-3 NIV). For further study to see how widespread the notion of sin causing affliction or death really was, see: 1 Kings 17:18 and John 9:1-3.

With incisive brevity ("I tell you, no!"), Jesus dispels the notion that people always suffer because of sin in their lives. Then he points out the necessity of ensuring that we do not become so mired in a pure academic curiosity with regard to why others suffer in this life, that we fail to ensure that we are right with God and turn from our sin, which if un-repented of leads to eternal suffering and banishment from God.

However, suffice it to say, God's Word affirms that there can be specific instances of severe disciplinary suffering that one may experience at times, such as:

A believer might suffer unnecessarily for being a meddler.

"If you suffer, it should not be as a murderer or thief or any other kind of criminal, or even as a meddler" (1 Pet. 4:15 NIV).

There may be distressing consequences to befriending an ill-tempered person, the snares associated with learning his ways.

"Do not make friends with a hot-tempered man, do not associate with one easily angered, or you may learn his ways and get yourself ensnared" (Prov. 22:24, 25 NIV).

There is the judgment of the sin unto death, which may result from bringing disrepute to the cause of Christ.

"There is a sin that leads to death" (1 Jn. 5:16 NIV).

Then there is the fearful matter of grieving the Holy Spirit. Note the following:

- Samson's defeat and blindness—Judges 13–16
- Suffering through foolish choices—Psalm 107:17
- Israel's regret and leanness of soul—Psalm 106:15
- Judah's exile for not obeying Sabbath regulations relating to fallow land—2 Chronicles 36:15–21

Does God Give Us More Than We Can Bear?[153]

Have you ever heard one believer attempt to comfort another believer, who is experiencing a difficult trial, with these words, "Cheer up, friend! The Lord will never allow you to be tempted beyond what you can bear"?

Pastor Sean M. Doyle provides us with a useful word of clarification that brings refreshing perspective on a truth that is often misunderstood. He notes:

As sincere as this sentiment may be, the counsel is in essence faulty, in that the context of 1 Corinthians 10:12–13, from which the seeming well-intentioned phrase originates, relates not to a Christian bearing up under a *trial* of faith, but rather, to his or her need of remaining vigilant in a season of *temptation*.

The truth is, according to the Apostle Paul in 2 Corinthians 1, God will sometimes allow us to experience more hardship than we can bear in a trial (*not temptation*), so that we might not rely on our own natural devices or strength, but rather, and solely upon God, who delivers us from deadly perils (2 Cor. 1:8–10), and who will continue to deliver.

What We May Always Know to Be True about God in Our Pain

The following biblical truths can help us to revisit what we know to be absolutely true and dependable about God.

1. God is good—"The Lord is good, a refuge in times of trouble. He cares for those who trust in Him" (Nah. 1:7 NIV).
2. God is love—"God is love. Whoever lives in love lives in God, and God in him" (1 Jn. 4:16 NIV).
3. God is righteous—"The Lord is righteous in all his ways and loving towards all he has made" (Ps. 145:17 NIV).
4. God is holy—"Holy, holy, holy is the Lord Almighty; the whole earth is full of His glory" (Isa. 6:3 NIV).
5. God is light; He has no moral imperfection or evil within—"God is light; in him there is no darkness at all" (1 Jn. 1:5 NIV).
6. God is intentional; his ways are never without design—"In him we were also chosen, having been predestined according to the plan of him who works out everything in conformity with the purpose of his will" (Eph. 1:11 NIV).
7. God will judge the world in righteousness and truth—"Will not the Judge of all the earth do right?" (Gen. 18:25 NIV).
8. God takes no pleasure in allowing grief in his world—"For he does not willingly bring affliction or grief to the children of men" (Lam. 3:32-33 NIV).
9. The Lord will not crush a wounded heart—"A bruised reed he will not break" (Isa. 42:3 NIV).
10. God will see that His people receive justice—"Will he keep putting them off? I tell you, he will see that they get justice, and quickly" (Lk. 18:7–8 NIV).

Record My Lament

Record my lament; list my tears on your
scroll— Are they not in your record?
Then my enemies will turn back when I call for help.
By this I will know that God is for me.
In God, whose word I praise, in the Lord,
whose word I praise—
In God I trust; I will not be afraid.
What can man do to me?
I am under vows to you, O God;
I will present my thank offerings to you.
For you have delivered me from death
And my feet from stumbling,
That I may walk before God in the light of life.
—Psalm 56:8–13 (NIV)

I come away with the absolute certainty that God has ordered my
steps and that God was there, even in the darkest moments of my life.
I know this as surely as I know I exist.
—Ravi Zacharias[154]

Suffering: A Sign of Displeasure or Approval?

Although suffering has traditionally been perceived as a sign of God's displeasure with sinners (cf. Job 4:7–8), suffering can equally be seen to be a sign of approval from the Lord for His children. As a refiner purifies silver, so the Lord refines His people through pruning His "branches," or disciplining His sons and daughters so that they may partake of His holiness and display his likeness and glory (Heb. 12:10).

In this regard, Piper observed: "(Jesus) knew that suffering would be the path in this age for making him most visibly supreme."[155]

The following references highlight the resultant benefits of suffering (pruning and discipline):

> "He will sit as a refiner and purifier of silver; he will purify the Levites and refine them like gold and silver. Then the Lord will have men who will bring offerings in righteousness" (Mal. 3:3 NIV).

> "While every branch that does bear fruit, he prunes so that it will be even more fruitful" (Jn. 15:2 NIV).

> "Not only so, but we also rejoice in our sufferings, because we know that suffering produces perseverance ..." (Rom. 5:3–5 NIV).

> "...so that the proof of your faith—being more precious than gold, which is perishable even though tested by fire— may be found to result in praise, glory and honor at the revelation of Jesus Christ" (1 Pet. 1:7 NASB).

> "If you are insulted because of the name of Christ, you are blessed" (1 Pet. 4:14 NIV).

"No discipline seems pleasant at the time, but painful. Later on, however, it produces a harvest of righteousness and peace for those who have been trained by it" (Heb. 12:11 NIV).

With prescient insight, MacDonald ably focuses in, not so much on the core of the redemptive transaction (which is justification and reconciliation), but at the core of our character, where by living out the constraints of a redeemed life, we may model justice.

> Christ died to save us, not from suffering, but
> from ourselves; not from injustice,
> far less from justice, but from being unjust ...
> —George MacDonald[156]

Consider Him Who Endured

Therefore, since we are surrounded by such a great cloud of witnesses, let us throw off everything that hinders and the sin that so easily entangles, and let us *run with perseverance* the race marked out for us.

Let us fix our eyes on Jesus, the author and perfecter of our faith, who for the joy set before him *endured the cross*, scorning its shame, and sat down at the right hand of the throne of God.

Consider him who *endured such opposition* from sinful men, so that you will not grow weary and lose heart.

—Hebrews 12:1–3 (NIV)

Examples of Righteous Individuals Who Suffered

When believers in Christ suffer, it is not uncommon for them to conclude at times that they are being judged (corrected or disciplined) by God for not having enough faith, or that they have sinned or have demonstrated unbiblical, worldly attitudes or actions.

One, of course, must not discount such factors or possibilities. However, these options do not of necessity represent a universal norm, nor are they to be considered the only dynamics involved, or reasons for which a Christian might suffer.

Though suffering may not be a daily occurrence, its eventuality in various forms is certain. David Lowery notes: "One of the many paradoxes of the Christian life is that the grace of God is most keenly experienced not in the best, but in what seem to be the worst times."[157]

Without intending to cause the reader any undue alarm or apprehension, it is nevertheless appropriate to mention that the Bible at times portrays suffering for a believer as something that is not entirely abnormal (2 Cor. 11:23–29; 1 Pet. 4:1).

Scripture also affirms that suffering and severe trials of our faith are not always the expression of divine displeasure, but that they can be instead an indication of God's intention to refine, to perfect within us the character of Christ and to use us for higher, nobler purposes. "He will sit as a refiner and purifier of silver; he will purify the Levites and refine them like gold and silver. Then the Lord will have men who will bring offerings in righteousness ..." (Mal. 3:3 NIV).

Old Testament Examples:

Joseph was sold into Egyptian slavery by his jealous brothers.

"But, God was with him and rescued him from all his troubles" (Acts 7:9–10 NIV).

Joseph, Daniel, Job, and many other Old Testament believers had suffered (sometimes rather harshly and unjustly—Heb. 11:32–40), and yet they were viewed as righteous before God. In some cases, no particular sin was ever indicated—not that they were sinless—but the intent was for us to see clearly that they were regarded as honorable individuals in God's sight (Ezek. 14:14). Note: "the world was not worthy of them" (Heb. 11:38a NIV).

It is also highly significant that each of these individuals was instrumental in God's hands to bring glory to Him and enrichment to others as a result of their obedience during their suffering. By virtue of their stories being retained for us in the Bible, ample evidence of their approved characters is noted and appreciated.

This Is the Answer[158]

One of the most difficult lessons Job learned was that if he could not comprehend the intricate workings of God in nature and the created order, how then could he possibly think he was entitled to stand in judgment as a critic of God's dealings with mankind in the realm of the spirit and heart?

Peter Kreeft explains further.

> God will not answer Job because God is not the *Answer Man* ...
> He is the Initiator, the Questioner, the Answer to everything.
> No one, not even Job, can ever be dissatisfied with this answer ...
>
> Then the Lord answered Job out of the whirlwind and said,
> Who is this that darkens counsel by words without knowledge?
> Now gird up your loins like a man,
> And I will ask you, and you instruct me!
> —Job 38:1-3 (NASB)

Old Testament Examples (cont'd)

Job's so-called comforters alleged that he suffered because of sin (Job 15:4-6), but he was proven to be a man of uprightness instead.

"Even if these three men—Noah, Daniel, and Job—were in it [in a country that sins, v. 13], they could save only themselves by their righteousness, declares the sovereign Lord" (Ezek. 14:14 NIV).

Jeremiah, who was placed into a muddy, dank cistern by his enemies (Jer. 38:6-10), pleaded for God's mercy and justice and was heard for his innocence.

"I called on your name, Lord, from the depths of the pit ... You came near when I called you, and you said, 'Do not fear,' "You, Lord, took up my case ... You have seen, O Lord, the wrong done to me" (Lam. 3:55, 57–59 NIV).

New Testament Examples:

To complement the above examples of suffering from the Old Testament, it is helpful to consider in particular the case of the following New Testament individuals who had clearly suffered within the context of God's will yet:

- They were not lacking in faith.
- They were not guilty of a particular or known sin.
- They had not been acting in a carnal or fleshly manner.

Stephen had great faith but was stoned to death.

"They chose Stephen, a man full of faith and of the Holy Spirit ... Now Stephen, a man full of God's grace and power, did great wonders and miraculous signs among the people" (Acts 6:5, 8 NIV).

Paul was an apostle, founder of churches, and author of much of the New Testament, and yet he was tormented by a thorn, which functioned like a messenger of Satan, his suffering for the gospel, not withstanding. (Please note: 2 Cor. 11:23-29; 2 Cor. 12:7-9, and Phil. 1:12).

"And because of the surpassing greatness of the revelations, for this reason, to keep me from exalting myself, there was given me a thorn in the flesh, a messenger of Satan to torment me, to keep me from exalting myself ... And He has said to me, 'My grace is sufficient for you, for power is perfected in weakness'" (2 Cor. 12:7, 9 NASB).

The Bible shows that God allowed this to happen to Paul for a twofold purpose: (a) that Paul might not be tempted to exalt (vaunt) himself because of his incredible spiritual privileges, and (b) so that he might understand from his own personal experience that God's grace is more than sufficient for all life's circumstances.

When the Will of God Is Dangerous[159]

Following God's will in a fallen world is inherently dangerous. Over and over in Scripture, Jesus teaches us that His disciples will suffer for following Him. Of course, we will avoid a lot of suffering by following Him. We will avoid the suffering of guilt, the suffering of self-destruction, of spending an eternity in hell. However, there are other kinds of suffering we will encounter because we are following Him. And He wants us to be clear about this. In fact, in 1 Peter it says, "Now who will harm you if you are eager to do what is good? But, even if you do suffer for doing what is right, you are blessed ... Keep your conscience clear, so that when you are maligned, those who abuse you for your good conduct in Christ may be put to shame. For it is better to suffer for doing good, if that should be God's will, than to suffer for doing evil."

So some suffering can clearly be God's will. It is not necessarily the suffering itself that is God's will, but rather, in a fallen world, following the will of God will generate suffering in our lives. In fact, there are two things that are always the will of God and always dangerous in a fallen world: telling the truth and loving needy people; which means, if my life of following Jesus does not feel dangerous, I should probably pause and check to see if it's Jesus I am following.

Doing what Jesus does—telling the truth and loving needy people—is inherently unsafe in a fallen world of lies and selfishness. As Christians, we have heard much about speaking the truth, so I would like to focus on the other dangerous activity that Jesus invites us all to do—loving needy people.

Jesus said all the teaching of the law and the prophets could be summed up in these two commands: loving God and loving our neighbor, especially our needy neighbor. 1 John 4:20 says, "For anyone who does not love his brother whom he has seen cannot love God whom he has not seen."

—Gary Haugen

"But remember the former days, when, after being enlightened, you endured a great conflict of sufferings, partly by being made a public spectacle through reproaches and tribulations..."

—Heb. 10:32-33 (NASB).

New Testament Examples (cont'd)

It is worth noting that when the Lord Jesus ministered on earth, he learned obedience from what He suffered (Heb. 5:8). In fact, His suffering *qualified* Him by personal experience to be a sympathetic and fully qualified high priest who is touched with the feeling of our infirmity (Heb. 4:14–16).

When a believer suffers, he or she may possibly become disheartened, bewildered, or even angry at God, especially when no plausible explanation is perceived. As His beloved children, we seem to think that God owes us an apology for allowing suffering to occur in our lives, as if He were accountable to us, or that He owed an explanation to us for His actions (note in Job 13:16–28 how Job sought an explanation from God for his affliction).

Again, one may recall from his or her reading of Job that God's questions posed to Job toward the end of the book, showed Job that if he could not fathom the wisdom of God behind the wonders of the physical creation, how then could he presume to critique God's dealings with him in the realm of the spiritual? It is at this point that we as believers would probably do well to exercise restraint, recall that we are at best undeserving recipients of grace, and therefore, resist the urge to think that we can presume upon God to explain to us why hardships arise.

Why a Believer May Suffer

We are identified with Christ, our Lord, who suffered. It is not surprising then to discover that a crucified head and a pampered body are incompatible.

"If the world hates you, keep in mind that it hated me first …" (Jn. 15:18 NIV); "Blessed are you when people insult you … because of me" (Matt. 5:11 NIV).

Suffering for a believer is the pathway for entering into the fellowship of Christ's sufferings at a truly intimate level. It also enables him or her to understand better the pulse of the Lord's heart. The apostle Paul wrote:

> "I want to know Christ and the power of his resurrection
> and the fellowship of sharing in his sufferings, becoming
> like him in his death" (Phil. 3:10 NIV).

Nancy Pearcy adds this helpful insight: "Given our fallen human nature, we typically do not really *sit* before the Lord until our legs are knocked out from under us by crises—sorrows, loss or injustice."[160]

To encourage a deeper awareness of and sensitivity toward others who suffer.

"Remember those in prison as if you were their fellow prisoners and those who are mistreated, as if you yourselves were suffering" (Heb. 13:3 NIV).

My Cry for Relief

The waters closed over my head,
and I thought I was about to be cut off.
I called on your name, O Lord, from the depths of the pit.
You heard my plea: "Do not close your ears to *my cry for relief.*"
You came near when I called you, and you said, "Do not fear."
O Lord, you took up my case; you redeemed my life.
You have seen, O Lord, the wrong done to me. Uphold my cause!
You have seen the depth of their vengeance, all their plots against me.
O Lord, you have heard their insults and all their plots against me—

—Lamentations 3:54–61 (NIV)

Why a Believer May Suffer (cont'd)

To better understand the passion of Christ's heart and extent of His loving care for us.

The apostle John, who suffered, when imprisoned for his faith, expressed this truth in the following verse: "How great is the love the Father has lavished on us, that we should be called children of God!" (1 Jn. 3:1 NIV).

To foster a deeper appreciation of and reliance on God's unfailing mercy and strength.

As Paul the apostle, who bore patiently with his thorn, wrote: "That is why, for Christ's sake, I delight in weaknesses, in insults, in hardships, in persecutions, in difficulties. For when I am weak, then I am strong" (2 Cor. 12:10 NIV).

> Whenever we are tempted to accuse God for an alleged wrongdoing, to ask where He was when we were hurting, or to feel it's time for a pity party, then perhaps it would be well for us to pause for a time-out. Taking a time-out will enable us to get a grip, refocus on reality, and in turn recall that it was on Calvary's cruel cross that God secured our salvation and reconciled the world to Himself through the vicarious and sacrificial suffering of the sinless Lamb of God, Jesus; yes, all of that agony was for us!

How Job Kept His Faith in the Crucible of Suffering

Phillip Yancey relates the account of a Scottish minister who did not understand how people facing a loss in their lives could abandon the faith. "'Abandon it for what?' he cried. 'You people in the sunshine *may* believe the faith, but we in the shadow *must* believe it. We have nothing else!'"[161]

When anyone sustains a great personal loss, it is not surprising to hear him or her ask, "Is it possible to stand upright when my world turns upside down?"

If anyone understood the dynamics associated with finding a way of standing upright in an upside-down world, it was most certainly the biblical character Job.

Although Job continued to ask many deep and significant questions related to his suffering (characterized by the staggering loss of his health, herds, children, and wealth), he nevertheless demonstrated by what he chose to do that a resolute and devout faith in the Lord is still possible for a believer who is suffering through loss, pain, and bewilderment.

He Who Jests[162]

> He jests at scars
> Who never felt a wound.
> —Shakespeare

Now if we are children, then we are heirs—heirs of God and co-heirs with Christ, if indeed we share in his sufferings in order that we may also share in his glory. I consider that our present sufferings are not worth comparing with the glory that will be revealed in us.

> —Rom. 8:17-18 (NIV)

How Job Maintained His Faith in the Crucible of Pain (cont'd)

❖ Job *Chose* to Worship

He was captivated by the wonder of God. Job blesses or praises God after his loss (showing implicit confidence in God's integrity of heart).

"Job got up and tore his robe ... then he fell to the ground *in worship* ..." (Job 1:20 NIV).

❖ Job *Confirmed* His Trust in the Trustworthy One

He cast himself upon God's trustworthiness. "Though he slay me, yet will I hope in him; I will surely defend my ways to his face" (Job 13:15 NIV).

❖ Job *Concentrated* on What Was Ahead

He was sustained in the present by a powerful, living hope in the future.

"I know that my redeemer lives, and that in the end he will stand upon the earth ... I myself will see him, with my own eyes—I, and not another" (Job 19:25, 27 NIV).

❖ Job *Correctly* Looked Beyond His Loss to the Gain

There was an outcome, but not necessarily an "out" from the painful process of refinement.

"I will *come forth* as gold" (Job 23:10 NIV).

❖ Job *Cast* Himself on God's Mercy in Repentance

He confessed his abysmal lack of understanding and consequent inability to critique God's ways and purposes for allowing this severe trial of faith.

"I know that you can do all things; no plan of yours can be thwarted ... My ears had heard of you, but now my eyes have seen you. Therefore, I despise myself and repent in dust and ashes" (Job 42:2, 5, 6 NIV).

Insight for Foresight:

In effect, one can safely infer from the above main points that unless there is a clear, overarching, and *redemptive* purpose to all of life, then there can be little, if any, meaningful reason at all for our existence.

Be Still, My Soul[163]

Be still, my soul—the Lord is on thy side! Bear patiently
the cross of grief or pain; Leave to thy God to order and
provide— In every change, He faithful will remain.
Be still, my soul—thy best, thy heavenly Friend
Through thorny ways, leads to a joyful end.

Be still, my soul—thy God doth undertake
To guide the future as He has the past;
Thy hope, thy confidence let nothing shake—
All now mysterious shall be bright at last.
Be still, my soul—the waves and winds still know
His voice who ruled them while He dwelt below.

Be still, my soul—the hour is hastening on
When we shall be forever with the Lord,
When disappointment, grief, and fear are gone,
Sorrow forgot love's purest joys restored.
Be still, my soul—when change and tears are past,
All safe and blessed we shall meet at last.

—Katharina Von Schlegel

Keeping the Glory Focus

Similarly, in 1 Peter, the apostle encouraged the believers of his day to look beyond what was going *against* them and to focus on what was going *for* them. Warren Wiersbe outlined Peter's words this way:[164]

- We are born for glory—"an inheritance ... kept in heaven for you" (1 Pet. 1:2–5 NIV).
- We are kept for glory—"who through faith are shielded by God's power until the coming of the salvation" (1 Pet. 1:5 NIV).
- We are prepared for glory—"so that your faith ... may be proved genuine and may result in praise, glory and honor ..." (1 Pet. 1:6–7 NIV).
- We may enjoy a foretaste of glory now—"and are filled with an inexpressible and glorious joy" (1 Pet. 1: 8–9 NIV).

Scripture Shows That Suffering for God's People Is Normal, Not Abnormal

"A righteous man may have many troubles" (Ps. 34:19 NIV).

"But join with me in suffering for the gospel" (2 Tim. 1:8 NIV).

"For which I am suffering, even to the point of being chained like a criminal" (2 Tim. 2:9 NIV).

"Everyone who wants to live a godly life in Christ Jesus will be persecuted" (2 Tim. 3:12 NIV).

"Endure hardship" (2 Tim. 2:3 NIV).

Oswald Chambers brings a helpful insight at this point when he says: "Choosing to suffer means that there must be something wrong with you, but choosing God's will—even if it means you will suffer—is something very different.

No normal, healthy saint ever chooses suffering; he simply chooses God's will, just as Jesus did, whether it means suffering or not."[165]

"But even if you should suffer for what is right, you are blessed."—1 Pet. 3:14 (NIV)

Sent to Try Us!¹⁶⁶

They say these things are *"sent to try us."*

But of course, one must take *"sent to try us"* the right way.

God has not been trying an experiment on my faith or love in order to find out their quality. He knew it already. It was I who didn't.

In this trial He makes us occupy the dock, the witness box, and the bench all at once. He always knew that my temple was a house of cards. His only way to make me realize the fact was to knock it down.

—C. S. Lewis

Consider it pure joy, my brothers and sisters, whenever you face trials of many kinds, because you know that the testing of your faith produces perseverance.

—Jam. 1:2-3

In Our Suffering, God Always Acts According to His Perfect Will and Integrity

❖ God is altogether righteous—"For the Lord is righteous, he loves justice; upright men will see his face" (Ps. 11:7 NIV).

❖ God is love—"And so we know and rely on the love God has for us. God is love" (1 Jn. 4:16 NIV).

❖ God is good—"The Lord is good, a refuge in times of trouble. He cares for those who trust in him ..." (Nah. 1:7 NIV).

❖ God gives good gifts—"How much more will your Father in heaven give good gifts to those who ask him" (Matt. 7:11 NIV).

❖ God is gentle—"A bruised reed he will not break, and a smoldering wick he will not snuff out" (Isa. 42:3 NIV).

❖ God is fully trustworthy—"So keep up your courage, men, for I have faith in God that it will happen just as he told me" (Acts 27:25 NIV).

❖ God's faithfulness endures to all generations—"Your faithfulness continues through all generations" (Ps. 119:90 NIV).

The Duration of Our Suffering Is Not Indefinite

"Though now for a little while you may have had to suffer grief in all kinds of trials" (1 Pet. 1:6 NIV).

"I consider that our present sufferings are not worth comparing with the glory that will be revealed in us" (Rom. 8:18 NIV).

"When he has tested me, I shall come forth as gold" (Job 23:10 NIV).

"After his suffering, He (Jesus) … gave many convincing proofs that he was alive" (Acts 1:3 NIV).

"The devil will put some of you in prison to test you, and you will suffer persecution for ten days. Be faithful, even to the point of death, and I will give you the crown of life" (Rev. 2:10-11 NIV).

"Weeping may remain for a night, but rejoicing comes in the morning" (Ps. 30:5 NIV).

Completely Honest With God[167]

One thing I often say to people for whom I am providing pastoral care, in the event of great loss and grief, is that that "there are no wrong emotions right now"... that God gave them their emotions, and he can handle whatever is coursing through their soul. Over time, healing needs to come, and God alone can truly bring this, but I believe people need to be free to truly express to God the fullness of the burden they are carrying. I'm reminded of the scripture in Hebrews "We can approach the throne of grace with confidence to find help in our time of need"... and part of that confidence is that we can be completely honest with God about our emotions and feelings in times of pain, grief, and loss.

Suffering for the Child of God Benefits the Soul

Contrary to the contentions from open theists, such as Sanders, who states that "God does not have a specific divine purpose for each and every occurrence of evil" (John E. Sanders, *The God Who Risks,* IVP),[168] suffering can be profitable for the believer and glorifying to God. Consider the following situations:

- ❖ Joseph in prison—"You intended to harm me, but God *intended* it for good to accomplish what is now being done, the saving of many lives" (Gen. 50:20 NIV).
- ❖ Hezekiah's illness—"Surely it was for my benefit that I suffered such anguish. In your love, you kept me from the pit of destruction; you have put all my sins behind your back" (Isa. 38:17 NIV).
- ❖ Paul's thorn—"To keep me from becoming conceited … there was given me a thorn in my flesh … to torment me …" (2 Cor. 12:7 NIV).
- ❖ Paul's imprisonment—"Now I want you to know, brothers, that what has happened to me has really served to advance the gospel" (Phil. 1:12–14 NIV).
- ❖ Man born blind—"'Neither this man nor his parents sinned,' said Jesus, 'but this happened so that the work of God might be displayed in his life'" (Jn. 9:3 NIV).
- ❖ The trials of our faith—"Perseverance must finish its work, so that you may be mature and complete, not lacking anything" (James 1:4 NIV).
- ❖ Our assessment of who God is—"Yet you know me, O Lord; You see me, and test my thoughts about you" (Jer. 12:1-3 NIV).

For forty-nine years, Charles Simeon served as the minister of Trinity Church in Cambridge, England. A friend once asked Simeon how he endured opposition to his ministry. Pastor Simeon replied:

My dear brother, we must not mind a little suffering for Christ's sake. When I am getting through a hedge, if my head and shoulders are safely through, I can bear the pricking of my legs. Let us rejoice in the remembrance that our holy Head has summoned all His suffering and triumphed over death. Let us follow Him patiently; we shall soon be partakers of His victory.[169]

Geisler and Turek concur. "If God prevented pain every time we got into trouble then we would become the most reckless, self-centered creatures in the universe. And we would never learn from suffering."[170]

Therefore, I will boast all the more gladly about my weaknesses, so that Christ's power may rest on me (2 Cor. 12:9 NIV).

I Will Trust and Not Be Afraid

In that day, you will say: "I will praise you, Lord.
Although you were angry with me,
Your anger has turned away and you have comforted me."
Surely God is my salvation;
I will trust and not be afraid.
The Lord, the Lord himself, is my strength and my song (defense);
He has become my salvation.
With joy you will draw water from the wells of salvation.

—Isaiah 12:1–3 (NIV)

Part IV
Dignity of the Dark Threads

And all the unknown joys He gives were
bought with agonies unknown.
—Isaac Watts[171]

Vale of Sorrow

I have been through the valley of weeping,
The *Vale of Sorrow* and Pain;
But, the God of all comfort was with me
At hand, to uphold and sustain.

—Author Unknown*

---

* This poem was popularized by Mrs. Charles E. Cowman, who featured it in her well-known *Streams in the Desert*.

The Dignity of the Dark Threads

Being blessed by others, who, passing through the
Valley of Baca, make it a well. —Psalm 84:6 (KJV)

My Life Is but a Weaving[172]

My life is but a weaving between my Lord and me; He chooses all the colors, and works on steadily.

Oft times He weaves sorrow and I, in blinded pride, Forget He sees the upper, and I the underside.

The dark threads are as needful in the Weaver's skillful hand, As the threads of gold and silver in the pattern He has planned.

Not till the loom is silent, and the shuttles cease to fly, Will God unroll the fabric, and show the reason why.

—"The Tapestry Poem," popularly attributed to Corrie Ten Boom

A Word of Introduction

In Hebrews, chapter 12, we read that Christians are surrounded or "encompassed about" by a vast host of believers from earlier ages, whom the Bible describes as a *cloud of witnesses*. These individuals, who by virtue of their having been kept by God during seasons of great trials to their faith in the past, now bear a resounding witness to us through the inspired record of their testimony to the enduring tender mercies of God in bearing His children up, even under the most extremely demanding or dangerous circumstances.

Now the awesome insights gained from a few new friends, who have walked with Jesus in our day, have been selected to feature in this section, because through their unique experiences, they clearly illustrate how utterly faithful God remains to those who trust Him. Their testimony points out that irrespective of the nature of one's trying circumstances, when one is utterly bereft of the natural, human ability to cope, God shows Himself to be the strength of our hearts (Ps. 73:26).

Selecting the title "The Dignity of the Dark Threads" was not difficult. In fact, it made perfect sense, in that it communicates to us that suffering is not of necessity a series of unrelated events or meaningless, arbitrary threads in the tapestry of life suggesting that believers are somehow left to the cruel whim of fate or to dangle in the wind.

Instead, the testimony ringing out over the ages (and in these pages) from the Lord's people, who have endured patiently through affliction at the coalface, is that they have been under the watchful eye of the master designer, who has and will continue to perfect within His children the very likeness of Christ's image (or character traits, Ps. 138:8; Rom. 8:29).

Therefore, since we have so great a cloud of witnesses surrounding us, let us also lay aside every encumbrance, and the sin which so easily entangles us, and let us run with endurance the race that is set before us, fixing our eyes on Jesus, the author and perfecter of faith, who for the joy set before Him endured the cross, despising the shame, and has sat down at the right hand of the throne of God. (Heb. 12:1–2 NASB)

Correction or Mercy?[173]

Let me think no degree of this thy correction casual, or
without signification, but yet when I have read it in that
language, as a correction, let me translate it into another,
and read it as a mercy; and which of these is the
original, and which is the translation;
whether thy mercy or thy correction were thy primary
and original intention in this sickness, I cannot conclude,
though death conclude me; for as it must necessarily
appear to be a correction, so I can have no greater
argument of thy mercy, than to die
in thee and by that death to be united to him who died for me.

—John Donne

Suffering with Christ, Reigning with Christ[174]

by Diane Hawkins

One of the ugliest evils perpetrated by man is the violation of innocence that occurs in child sexual abuse. The damaging effects set in motion by this hideous sin can last for decades, permeating many facets of the victim's life. It is against this challenging backdrop that I have gradually come to see the hand of God actively working in love to comfort, strengthen, restore, and bring awesome hope into my life.

For over 15 years my father involved me in a child sex ring, producing hard-core child pornography and pimping me to other men for purposes of financial gain. This began so early in life that my immature psyche separated these intolerable acts into sequestered parts of my mind, beyond the reach of conscious recall. There they silently remained until being poignantly stirred to life again when I entered the pure and holy sexual experience of the marriage bed.

As this brutal awakening to the realities of my past occurred, grappling with how my own father could have so utterly betrayed me was hard enough. Comprehending why my Heavenly Father allowed me to suffer such unjust and perverted abuse was even more difficult.

As I sank into deep depression, I felt totally deserted by God—until one day, in listening to a tape by David Needham, God opened my eyes to the fact that He desires to use suffering for good purposes in our lives.

Instantly buoyed by this new revelation, I began an earnest study of Scripture for all the good things He can accomplish in the lives of His children through suffering. In the end my list included:

1. To chasten for sin (Heb. 12:5–11; 1 Pet. 4:1–2).
2. To test our faith (James 1:2–3; 1 Pet. 1:6–7; 4:12; Job 23:10; Isa. 48:10).
3. To build our faith (2 Cor. 1:8–9).
4. To build our character (Rom. 5:3–4; James 1:2–4; 1 Pet. 5:10; Heb. 2:10).
5. To gain a greater knowledge or experience of God (Job 42:5; Ps. 56:8; Rom. 8:17; Eph. 1:19–20; Phil. 3:8–10; 1 Pet. 4:13; cf. Col. 1:24).
6. To show the greatness of God's power
   a. In removing the cause of the suffering (Jn. 9:2ff).
   b. In working through man in spite of his afflictions (2 Cor. 4:7), to demonstrate His sufficient grace (2 Cor. 12:9–10), and to bring the Gospel to the unsaved (Acts 16:19–34; Phil. 1:12–13; 2 Tim. 2:8–10).
7. To enable us to comfort others (2 Cor. 1:3–4).
8. To demonstrate to the spiritual realm the strength of man's faith in God (Job) and the sufficiency of God's grace.

(Cont'd on following pages)

When You Cry for Help

Yet the Lord longs to be gracious to you; He
rises to show you compassion.
For the Lord is a God of justice. Blessed are all who wait for him!

O people of Zion, who live in Jerusalem, you will weep no more.
How gracious he will be *when you cry for help*!
As soon as he hears, he will answer you.

Although the Lord gives you the bread of
adversity and the water of affliction,
your teachers will be hidden no more;
with your own eyes, you will see them.

Whether you turn to the right or to the left, your ears will hear
a voice behind you, saying, "This is the way; walk in it."
—Isaiah 30:18–21 (NIV)

Even with this insight, however, I still wrestled with the nature of the suffering God had seemingly allowed into my life and how I could reconcile that with His love. This began an even deeper journey of discovery for me. In the end, I was more impacted than ever with how much God truly loves me and longs to be united with me in an everlasting and all-fulfilling love relationship. I also gained a better grasp of God's overall plan to accomplish this goal, including His creation of Satan as an alternative object of devotion for man.

God knew that implementing His plan would bring evil into the human race. He knew that this would mean suffering—for both man and Himself. While the price was high, He viewed competition as a critical factor that would strengthen the love bond He so greatly desired with those who would choose Him. He also knew that through suffering, love develops a sterling quality. Therefore, with the joy of this awesome love relationship set before Him (His "glorious inheritance," Eph. 1:18 NIV), Jesus willingly embraced the suffering required on His part to redeem man from Satan's dominion (Col.1:13; Heb. 12:2). Sadly, many who so easily utter the words "Jesus died for my sins" fall far short of comprehending the costly nature of this act. Feeling compelled to spend 40 days studying the crucifixion, I emerged thoroughly convinced that no human being has ever borne the degree of *physical, emotional,* and *spiritual* suffering that Jesus endured on the cross of Calvary as He bore the sins of the whole world, throughout history, *all at once.*

When my own suffering was brought into the context of this bigger picture and I could see the love of God so strongly demonstrated in both the goal for which He had allowed evil to come into the world and in the suffering that Jesus Himself endured to accomplish this goal, my cries of protest were silenced. Instead, I humbly relinquished myself to join in the "fellowship of [Jesus'] sufferings" (Phil. 3:10 KJV), understanding for the first time what this really meant. As I united my heart with His plan, I essentially declared my willingness to accept the consequences of evil that lie in *my* path as, together, we eagerly anticipate the goal ahead.

Several years later God used Revelation 12:11 to open my eyes to the poignant realization that the ultimate act of entering into the sufferings of Christ is to die a martyr's death. Far from being a tragic waste of human life, however, God impressed upon me that such deaths actually play a significant role in seemingly releasing spiritual power for the final defeat of Satan— just as Jesus' death did in an infinitely greater manner (Eph. 4:8–10; Col. 2:15). In another major upheaval of perspective, I no longer see martyrdom as a horrible tragedy, but as a high honor for a Christian soldier in the kingdom of God.

With this insight, God shifted my focus to a whole new aspect of His love in the big picture He was painting for me. I quickly recognized that His sovereignty allows Him to have the final say in *any* act of evil perpetrated against us. Therefore, as His grace-giving presence surrounds us in our times of suffering, His love-saturated justice takes account of every tear we shed and is poised *to compensate us for each one* (Ps. 56:8; 2 Cor. 12:9; Heb. 13:5)!

This recompense may begin even in this life (Gen. 50:20; Rom. 8:28), but it will occur most fully in heaven, where the glory we share with Christ will seemingly increase according to the degree of suffering we have experienced on earth (Rom. 8:18). Those who faithfully enter the fellowship of Christ's sufferings will also share in the privilege of reigning with Him in His eternal kingdom (2 Tim. 2:12). What joy we will experience when on that great day, we exchange our suffering for a crown and enter into the fullness of our reward, the perfect love relationship with God for which He created us!

God Is Reigning Today[175]

And I beheld, and lo, in the midst of the throne and of the four beasts... stood a Lamb as it had been slain —Rev. 5:6 (KJV)

> God is reigning today ... Where He does not rule, He overrules, and His purposes are going to be fulfilled.
>
> Imagine if you will this old man (Apostle John) who had faithfully served Christ, now alone in exile, suffering for his faith. And yet, when he writes a book, it is not about himself and his trials; it is about Jesus Christ and His triumphs.
>
> He does not write, "Woe is me, Caesar is on the throne." That's not the language of faith! No, John writes, "Hallelujah: for the Lord God Omnipotent (almighty) reigns (Rev. 19:6)!"
>
> —Warren W. Wiersbe

> Thy kingdom is an everlasting kingdom,
> and thy dominion endureth throughout all generations
> —Ps. 145:13 (KJV)

> There are rare and wonderful species of joy that flourish
> only in the rainy atmosphere of suffering.
> —J. Piper[176]

In light of Piper's articulate commentary, we should not be surprised then to read in Hebrews 12 that Jesus, for the joy that was set before him, endured the cross and despised its shame.

Peculiarly Dreadful Things[177]

So, it is to live in the experience of faith that if God calls us
unto any of those things which are peculiarly dreadful unto our
natures, He will give us such supplies of spiritual strength and
patience as shall enable us to undergo them, if not with ease and
joy, yet with peace and quietness beyond our expectation.

—John Owen

Come Thou Fount[178]

by Harry Adams

Recently my wife and daughter and I were reading Psalm 37. When we came to the fourth verse "Delight yourself in the Lord and he will give you the desires of your heart" I asked if this was true for me.

I am crippled by Lou Gehrig's disease, ALS, which is a progressive and fatal neurological illness. In the eight years that I've had ALS it's taken my voice and robbed me of the use of my limbs. It also forced us out of our lovely home.

Is the promise of fulfilled desires true for me and for the millions of other believers who have had their plans and dreams shattered?

Yes, it's true—exceedingly so.

* ❖ I desire a healthy body, and He promises me a body that is powerful, incorruptible, glorious and spiritual.
* ❖ I desire a home that is beautiful and spacious, and He is preparing such a home for me in a city whose builder is God.
* ❖ I desire a world without crime, lies or violence, and He promises me a world where righteousness dwells.
* ❖ I desire to be with those I love, and He promises that I will be caught up together with them forever.
* ❖ I desire an end to my sorrow, and He promises me fullness of joy in His presence.

During That Long Period

During that *long period*, the king of Egypt died. The Israelites
groaned in their slavery and *cried out*, and their cry for help,
because of their slavery, went up to God.
God heard their groaning and
he remembered his covenant with Abraham,
with Isaac and with Jacob.
So *God looked* on the Israelites and was *concerned about them*.
—Exodus 2:23–25 (NIV)

❖ I desire a heart so filled with love that there is no room for sin, and He promises to make me like Jesus when I am in heaven.

❖ I desire a ministry, and He promises I will serve Him eternally.

❖ I desire a voice with which to praise Him, and He promises I will sing before His throne.

❖ Most of all, I desire to see Him, and He promises I will always behold His face.

> He will keep His promise to give me the desires of my heart.

Reproduced from *Kindred Spirit*, summer 2005, vol. 29, no. 2. Used with Permission from KS and Mrs. Susan Adams.

Editorial note: Subsequent to the telling of Harry Adams's story, he was promoted to glory in 2008. The reader may find Romans 8:18 to be a perfect summation of the hope that sustained Harry Adams and family through their personal ordeal.

The great French painter Pierre Renoir gradually became crippled by arthritis and was eventually confined to a wheelchair. Although his hands were twisted and deformed, he still continued to paint. He could hold the brush only with his fingertips, and he endured excruciating agony with every stroke. Henri Matise, a fellow artist, watching him at work, asked, "How can you paint at the expense of such torture?" Renoir replied, "The pain passes, but the beauty remains!"[179]

Jesus Draw Me Ever Nearer[180]

Music by Keith Getty
Words by Margaret Becker

Jesus draw me nearer
As I labour through the storm.
You have called me to this passage,
And I'll follow, though I'm worn.

May this journey bring a blessing;
May I rise on wings of faith;
And at the end of my heart's testing,
With your likeness let me wake.

Jesus guide me through the tempest;
Keep my spirit staid and sure.
When the midnight meets the morning,
Let me love You even more.

Let the treasures of the trial
Form within me as I go—
And at the end of this long passage,
Let me leave them at Your throne.

A Survivor's Account of the Events of 9/11—WTC[181]

By George W. Sleigh

(With Stephen Sleigh)

It was 8:47 a.m. on Tuesday September 11th 2001, and I was at my desk on the north wall of Building 1 of the World Trade Center (WTC). I had been out of the office on Monday and I was catching up with my email and telephone messages. I called our Cleveland office for a phone number I needed to obtain information for a scheduled 3:00 p.m. meeting with a client (Oshima Shipyard). During the course of our conversation I heard an unusually loud roar from outside the building and, looking out the window, saw a large commercial jet headed right towards us. I was not able to identify the airline or model of the plane, but I did observe that the wheels were up and the thought that passed through my mind was "This guy is kind of low"! Almost immediately, the airplane struck the building above me and to my right.

As soon as I heard the crash of the plane, the surroundings of my office came loose, and I was covered with ceiling tiles, light fixtures, cubicle bookshelves and contents, etc. I had crouched forward in my chair, covered my head and prayed for God's protection. I had no sense of any movement in the building and there was no indication of any broken windows and no apparent major structural damage in our area. Steve McIntyre, one of my colleagues rushed to see if I was OK, and, replying in the affirmative I then crawled out from under the debris.

We gathered together to ensure that all the employees known to be in the office at the time were accounted for, and then we decided to evacuate from the building immediately. Realizing that my briefcase contained my address / telephone book I crawled back into my work area, retrieved the brief case and headed out of the office.

Merline Mayers, one of our employees, handed each of us a section of paper towel, which had been soaked in water to protect our breathing from the smoke, and we headed for the stair towers. Two of the stair towers were blocked and the third one was blocked above us with some debris below. We entered this stairwell, clearing the debris as we went and headed down. There was about an inch of water on the initial flights of stairs but this stopped rather quickly and the subsequent flights were dry and well lit. Several floors down we encountered Port Authority personnel, who directed us through their office to a more suitable stairway.

During this transition, we were soaked by a number of fire hoses that were running and it was at this point that looking up through the ceiling I saw flames and began to realize the seriousness of our situation.

Our progress down this second stairway was orderly and fairly rapid with only occasional slowdowns to allow for passage of a number of individuals being assisted in their descent. The 11 of us that had left our office together were gradually separated and Dick Anderson and I brought up the rear of our group on our journey down. About every 10 floors or so there were Port Authority personnel directing and encouraging us to keep moving and to hold on to the handrails as the stairs were becoming slippery.

He Brings Them Out

Then they cry unto the Lord in their trouble, and
he brings them out of their distresses. He makes the
storm a calm, so that the waves thereof are still.

—Psalm 107:28–29 (KJV)

As we approached the lower floors, the volume of people in the stairway increased, causing a slowdown in our descent rate and a few times we came to a complete halt for one or two minutes at a time. There was, however, no panic or pushing and we continued down. Occasionally we had to move to the right to make way for the firemen coming up. We felt sorry for them as they were carrying maybe 50/60 lbs of equipment including their protective clothing, helmets, axes, hoses, oxygen tanks, etc. It was only after the full extent of the attack was apparent that I realized that many of these men probably would not have made it out before the building collapsed.

Over the last few flights of stairs, I had moved ahead of Dick (he probably stopped to talk with someone about the Red Sox!) and finally exited the stairwell at the mezzanine level and was horrified to see the extent of the damage. Looking out on the plaza there were mounds of burning rubble everywhere; inside the building all the façade had been blown off the walls and the glass in the partition walls between Tower 1 and the concourse was shattered. I was directed down a (now) stationary escalator to the concourse level and then east through the concourse to the building exits.

Commended by God

For it is commendable if someone bears up under the pain
of unjust suffering because he is conscious of God.

But how is it to your credit if you receive a beating for
doing wrong and endure it? But if you suffer for doing good
and you endure it, this is commendable before God.
—1 Peter 2:19—20 (NIV)

Passing through the initial portion of the concourse and on towards the PATH train escalators, the overhead sprinklers were on, and I became soaked from head to toe as there was about six inches of standing water on the floor. I passed the coffee shop on my left and was heading towards The Gap when there was a tremendous explosion from the direction of Tower 2. Looking back in that direction, I noted that the spray from the sprinklers was now horizontal and I observed large objects flying by at high speed.

I immediately started to run away from the direction of the blast and then found myself enveloped in darkness and in a huge cloud of dust and debris. The thought that went through my mind was "so this is how my life is going to end." However, I was not afraid but cried out to God to save me. I was able to maintain my footing and was propelled across the concourse until I came to a stop in a doorway, the frame of which appeared to be intact. I thanked God for sparing me so far and decided that this was a good place to stay until things settled down. For the second time that morning, large portions of the overhead had collapsed around me and I could feel what appeared to be aluminum support beams, maybe 6" by 3", and recalled watching these being installed a few years ago. After hearing a few crashing sounds overhead, it became eerily silent.

As the dust settled I was able to see a solitary overhead light still burning and walked over to it. I called out to find if there was anyone else in the vicinity and two men came over to me. Together we called out a few times and were heard by Port Authority personnel who had been directing people out of the building. We walked over to them, directed by their flashlights, and they proceeded to direct us out of the building. We exited through building 5 onto the plaza and from there across Church Street and up Fulton Street to Broadway. At no time did I look back towards the Towers; if I had, I would have seen that Tower 2 had collapsed, which explains the explosion that occurred when I was in the concourse. At this time, I noticed that the right leg of my pants was soaked in blood. I had no recollection of being hit although my right knee and left ankle felt as though I had twisted them. However, I guess the adrenaline was in high gear and I walked as rapidly as possible away from the WTC.

Our God, Our Help[182]

"St. Anne"

by Sir Isaac Watts

1) Our God, our help in ages past,
Our Hope for years to come,
Our shelter from the stormy-blast,
And our eternal home!

2) Under the shadow of Thy throne
Still may we dwell secure;
Sufficient is Thine arm alone,
And our defense is sure.

3) Before the hills in order stood,
Or earth received her frame,
From everlasting Thou art God,
To endless years the same.

4) A thousand ages in your sight
are like an evening gone,
short as the watch that ends the night
before the rising sun.

5) Time, like an ever-rolling stream,
soon bears us all away;
we fly forgotten,
as a dream dies at the opening day.

6) Our God, our help in ages past,
Our hope for years to come,
Be thou our guide while life shall last,
And our eternal home. Amen

There were numerous photographers taking pictures of us at the top of Fulton Street, but I paid little attention to them and turned north on Broadway. One of the pictures taken was in many of the London (UK) newspapers the next day, and my son Stephen says he wept when he opened the *Daily Telegraph* and saw my picture there.

A police officer handed me a bottle of water and told me to rinse out my eyes and mouth. He then directed me to an EMT vehicle. As I climbed in along with an elderly lady, he told the driver to "get moving, the building is collapsing". We took off and were directed to Beth Israel Hospital on the corner of 1st Avenue and 16th Street. The EMT technician gave me oxygen, and then bandaged the lacerations on my right leg. He also told us of the plane flying in to Tower 2 and of the attack on the Pentagon. This was the first indication I had that this was something other than an accident.

Upon arrival at the hospital I was directed to an outdoor shower (which fortunately was warm water) and, still fully dressed, cleaned off as much as possible of the accumulated dust. Immediately after showering, I tried to call Elaine to let her know that I was safe. However, cell phones were not working and the land lines were all busy. I was then pushed in a wheelchair though the triage area, into the Emergency Treatment Centre. The hospital staff members were incredibly efficient and caring, and taking me to a treatment cubicle immediately examined the lacerations on my right leg. I removed my shoes and socks and noticed a deep laceration on the inside of my left leg at the ankle. This was open all the way to the bone and, apologizing for the lack of any local anesthesia the medical staff washed out my wounds and stapled them closed.

After being discharged from the Emergency Centre I ended up in a waiting area where there were a couple of pay phones. I sat there for about 45 minutes trying to get through and finally at 12:00 p.m. I was successful! One of Elaine's co-workers (Carol Megaro) answered and called her to the phone. I was so thrilled to hear her voice and to let her know the Lord had protected me!

There was no way to get out of Manhattan that night, so I spent the night and part of the next day in the Linsky Pavilion of the hospital, until Jerry Pinkard (retired ABS driver), was able to come in and take me home for a joyful reunion with Elaine.

So many people had called to let us know they were praying for us from the moment they knew of the attack. I am so thankful to God for his sovereignty and goodness in sparing my life and sparing my loved ones from the inexpressible sorrow that many thousands of others have gone through. Praise be to Him.

The following is from George's son, Stephen.

I find comfort and strength from the following verse from the Psalms.

> "The Lord is my light and my salvation—whom shall I fear? The Lord is the stronghold of my life—of whom shall I be afraid? When evil men advance against me to devour my flesh, when my enemies and my foes attack me, they will stumble and fall. Though an army besiege me, my heart will not fear; though war break out against me, even then will I be confident" (Psalm 27:1–3 NIV).

May God, bless you and be with you.

Fruitfulness in Suffering

Joseph named his firstborn Manasseh, and said, "It is because God
has made me forget all my trouble and all my father's household."
The second son he named Ephraim and said, "It is because
God has made me *fruitful in the land of my suffering*."
—Genesis 41:51–52 (NIV)

To This You Were Called

To this you were called, because Christ suffered for you, leaving
you an example that you should follow in his steps.
"He committed no sin, and no deceit was found in his mouth."
When they hurled their insults at him, he did not
retaliate; when he suffered, he made no threats. Instead,
he entrusted himself to him who judges justly.

—1 Peter 2:21—23

Blessed Assurance[183]

By Joseph Stowell

Fanny Crosby knew about suffering. In the 1800s, this prolific poet wrote hundreds of gospel songs and Christian hymns.

If you examine her lyrics closely, you can see the grid of personal experience through which her memorable words emerge.

Fanny Crosby was blind, but not from birth. Doctors had made a tragic mistake in prescribing the wrong eye drops when she was an infant. She spent the rest of her life unable to see. It has been widely reported that Mrs. Crosby often said she was glad to be visually impaired, since it would mean that the first thing she would see was the person of Jesus.

Unlike many victims of loss, who may feel every right to be bitter, Fanny's attitude (and fountain pen) articulated a spirit of mercy and love.

In one of her hymns, we have a clue to her ability to face suffering with confidence:

> "Angels descending bring from above, echoes
> of mercy, whispers of love."

Fanny Crosby knew a blessed assurance that originated in heaven.

Beyond the Losses[184]

It's not uncommon for friends to feel abandoned in the midst of their personal nightmare and trials of faith.

Dennis DeHaan assures us that our God is ever there for us.

> *Beyond the losses* of this life
> That cause us to despair
> New hope is born within our heart
> Because our God is there.
> —Dennis DeHaan

> They will bow down before you and plead with you saying, 'Surely God is with you, and there is no other; there is no other god.'
> —Isa. 45:14 (NIV)

From Bereavement to Blessing¹⁸⁵

Lettie B. Cowman was born in 1870 in the American state of Iowa. At nineteen years of age, she married Charles, who was one of the cofounders of the Oriental Missionary Society (now known as OMS International), along with E. Kilbourne and J. Nakada.

In 1901, the Cowmans responded to God's call to serve as missionaries in Japan. They served alongside their friend, Juji Nakada, whom they had met in Chicago.

After only two years, the ministry in Japan had advanced to such a degree that two Bible training institutes were founded to train up and nurture new believers.

It was clear that all cofounders of OMS had a God-given burden for the spiritual needs of the Japanese. This burden fostered the beginning of what became known as the Great Village Campaign in 1913. The goal of the campaign was for every person in Japan to hear the Gospel message. To help fulfill this vision, missionaries were sent out to every home throughout Japan, proclaiming the Gospel and distributing Bibles.

When Charles's health began to fail in 1917, he and Lettie returned to America. Not long after the Cowmans returned to America, they received news that the Great Village Campaign had been completed. Amazing as it may seem, nearly sixty million Japanese had heard the Gospel during this campaign, without the benefit of mass transportation, the Internet, or social media.

Unfortunately, owing to further incidents of heart attacks, Charles's health continued to decline. As he suffered, Lettie also felt his pain. It was during this time that God lead her to begin composing her best-selling devotional book, *Streams in the Desert*. Lettie wrote her devotional based on her hardships and her experiences with God's grace.

Interestingly, her publisher felt that when the book was initially printed, they would not publish more than three thousand copies. However, God had other plans, and the book soon became a worldwide best seller. Regarding her book, Mrs. Cowman once commented to the effect that, "I was not the author of *Streams*; it was God who gave it to me."

With his mission on earth completed, Charles Cowman was promoted to glory in September 1924. After his death, Lettie found a note addressed to her in his Bible, stating, "Go on with my unfinished task." Despite her sorrow and loss, Lettie understood she had further work to accomplish. Not long after Charles's death, Mr. Kilbourne also died, and Lettie became the third president of OMS, whilst maintaining an active writing and speaking ministry for the next thirty-three years.

However, in spite of her administrative commitments and age, she continued to feel not only the constraint to reach every home in Japan with the Gospel, but also the world. It has been noted that before the Nazis ascended to power in Europe, Mrs. Cowman's Gospel thrust throughout the continent represented one of the greater evangelistic efforts seen in Europe for that era.

After a three-year illness, Lettie B. Cowman, missionary stateswoman, passed into the presence of her Lord and savior on Easter Sunday, of all days, on April 17, 1960, at ninety years of age.

Comfort Is On Its Way![186]

God has come to wipe away our tears ... He is doing it;
He will have it done as soon as He can ... And until He can,
He would have them flow without bitterness ...
To which end He tells us
It is a blessed thing to mourn
Because of the *comfort That is on its way.*

—George MacDonald

Blessed are those who mourn,
for they will be comforted.

—Mt. 5:4

The Community of Grace[187]

by Gerald Sittser

It has often been stated that God does not necessarily comfort us to make us comfortable, but that we might be comforters. Sittser explains the significance of this concept when he writes:

> Loss is a universal experience ... But loss does not have to isolate us or make us feel lonely. Though it is a solitary experience we must face alone, loss is also a common experience that can lead us to community. It can create a community of brokenness. We must enter the darkness of loss alone, but once there we will find others with whom we can share life together.
>
> Community does not simply happen spontaneously, except in rare circumstances when conditions are right ...
>
> It requires a choice on the part of those who want to provide community for suffering friends. They must be willing to be changed by someone else's loss, though they might not have been directly affected by it.
>
> Comforters must be prepared to let the pain of another become their own and so let it transform them.

If we are distressed it is for your comfort...
which produces in you patient endurance of
the same sufferings we suffer
—2 Cor. 1:6

Meaning of Our Trials[188]

Life presents us with many seemingly, unsolvable mysteries. One of the mysteries that remain unsolved is why a good God will allow the trial of hardship to intrude itself upon the life of a dedicated, faithful believer.

Edersheim provides us with a helpful perspective on this matter.

> We cannot understand the meaning of many trials; God does not explain them. To explain a trial would be to destroy its object, which is that of calling forth faith and obedience.
> —Alfred Edersheim

> Because you know that the testing of your faith produces perseverance —Jam. 1:3 (NIV)

For His Time[189]

by David Roper

When South African pastor Andrew Murray was visiting England in 1895, he began to suffer pain from a previous back injury. While he was recuperating, his hostess told him of a woman who was in great trouble and wanted to know if he had any counsel for her. Murray said, "Give her this paper which I have been writing for my own (encouragement). It may be that she will find it helpful."

This is what Murray wrote:

"In time of trouble say:

First—God brought me here. It is by His will I am in this strait place. In that I will rest.

Next—He will keep me in His love and give me grace in this trial to behave as His child.

Then—He will make the trial a blessing, teaching me lessons He intends me to learn, and working in me the grace He means to bestow.

Last—In His good time He can bring me out again—how and when, He knows.

I am here—by God's appointment, in His keeping, under His training for His time."

We want the instant solution, the quick fix, but some things cannot be disposed of so readily; they can only be accepted. God will keep us by His love. By His grace, we can rest in Him.

A Little While![190]

> I consider that our present sufferings are not worth
> comparing with the glory that will be revealed in us—
> Rom. 8:18 (NIV)

F.B. Meyer reminds us that there is a limit to the duration of our suffering.

It is only for a little while, but every moment has been fixed by the immutable purpose and love of God. You shall not suffer one moment more than is absolutely necessary for your perfecting of God's glory, and for every moment there is an ample supply of grace.

> For our momentary, light affliction is producing for us an eternal
> weight of glory far beyond all comparison —2 Cor. 4:17 (NASB)

"O, Love That Will Not Let Me Go!"[191]

When we experience the wonder of God's transforming love, we come to appreciate how utterly limitless and steadfast it is. Dr. Joe Stowell relates how God's amazing love impacted the life and ministry of George Matheson.

On the evening of June 6, 1882, George Matheson wrote a classic, timeless hymn in the manse of Innelan. Its opening words are these:

> *"Oh, love that will not let me go, I rest my weary soul in Thee; I give Thee back the life I owe, that in Thine ocean depths its flow may richer, fuller be."*

What ultimately lead to the composition of this famous hymn was the fact that Matheson, who by the time he had turned eighteen, had completely lost his sight. On that particular day he had also been reflecting on the events of that day (it was his sister's wedding). He wrote, "I was at the time alone (Matheson's fiancé had also recently broken off their engagement). Something happened to me, which was known only to myself, and which caused me the most severe mental suffering."

Despite these setbacks, Matheson remained an outstanding student of God's Word and eventually became an effective preacher in the Church of Scotland. Much of his progress can be attributed to his sister, who even learned Hebrew and Greek in order to help her brother.

This famous hymn, "O Love That Will Not Let Me Go," was the fruit of that suffering. In the darkness of his blindness George Matheson found comfort in God's love.

—Joe Stowell

Do Not Fear

So, *do not fear*, for I am with you;
Do not be dismayed, for I am your God.
I will strengthen you and help you;
I will uphold you with my righteous right hand.
For I am the Lord, your God,
Who takes hold of your right hand,
And says to you, *do not fear*;
I will help you.
—Isaiah 41:10, 13 (NIV)

The Bass Notes of Our Life Song[192]

by Ruth Myers

I found immense comfort as I expressed to the Lord my grief at losing my loved one, and then let Him speak words of love to my heart. Words like the first part of Isaiah 43:4: "You are precious in my eyes, and honored, and I love you" (RSV).

Then I'd tell Him how glad I was that I still had my *Most Beloved One* with me: "Thank you Lord, that I can enjoy your love—the best love of all! Your love is intensely personal; it never fails."

As my human aloneness pressed me to love and adore the Lord in new ways, He gave me joy in the midst of sorrow. As C.H. Spurgeon wrote, "our grief cannot mar the melody of our praise; they are simply the bass notes of our life song, *To God Be the Glory!*"

I love the Lord, because he hears, (and continues to hear)
my voice and my supplications.
—Ps. 116:1 (AMP)

The Quelling of a Thousand Foes[193]

Oh, I Have Seen the Day When with a Single Word
God Helping Me to Say My Trust is in the Lord
My Soul Has Quelled a Thousand Foes
Fearless of All That Could Oppose.

—William Cowper

The Lord is my light and my salvation—whom shall I
fear? —Ps 27:1 (NIV)

Thanksgiving[194]
by Hannah Whitall-Smith

Hannah Whitall-Smith reminds of the importance of maintaining an attitude of a grateful heart.

Thanksgiving or complaining—these words express two contrasting attitudes of the souls of God's children in regard to His dealings with them; and they are more powerful than we are inclined to believe in furthering or frustrating His purposes of comfort and peace toward us. The soul that complains can find comfort in nothing.

We cannot always give thanks for all things themselves, but we can always give thanks for God's love and care in the things that touch our lives. Not one thing can touch us except with His knowledge and permission. He is in them somewhere, and He is in them to compel, even the most grievous, to work together for our good and His glory.

It is not because things are good that we are to thank the Lord, but because He is good. We are not wise enough to judge as to things, whether they are really in their essence, joys or sorrows. But we always know that the Lord is good, and that His goodness makes it absolutely certain that everything He provides or permits must be good; and must therefore be something for which we would be heartily thankful, if only we would see it with His eyes.

God invites us to enter His presence with thanksgiving and His courts with praise (Psalm 100). Could it be that giving thanks is the key that opens these gates more quickly than anything else?

> Enter His gates with thanksgiving and His courts with praise.
> Give thanks to Him, and praise His name. Ps. 100:4 (NIV)

The Powerlessness of Pain[195]

We should learn to ask God for things which are suitable for us to ask. For neither the splendours nor the pains of the present life have much power in respect either to despondency or pleasure; they are contemptible and slip away very swiftly. By their very nature, they do not long endure, but the things which are to come endure eternally, both those of punishment and those of the kingdom.

Let us then in regard to these things use much diligence to avoid the first and to choose the last. For what is the advantage of this world's luxury? Today it is, and tomorrow it is not; today a bright flower, tomorrow smoldering ashes. But spiritual things are not so; they ever remain shining and blooming, and becoming brighter every day.

—Phillip Schaff

Real Peace—Real Security[196]
by Millie Stamm

Many children have a "security blanket" which they have to take to bed with them. It may be a real blanket, a stuffed animal, or some toy. It is something they can tightly clutch in their arms to give a feeling of security and confidence.

As never before, fear is gripping the hearts of millions in the world today. In such an age when people's hearts are failing them for fear, many of us have *security blankets* to which we desperately clutch; something to give a sense of safety in a frightening world.

Some people turn to tranquilizers, alcohol, and drugs. But these do not bring permanent peace of heart and mind. The Bible often admonishes us not to fear, "Be not afraid of sudden fear" (Prov. 3:25).

A confidence that releases us from fear comes from peace of mind and heart and it comes from being at peace with God through Jesus Christ. Someone has said, "We think security brings peace—*but real peace brings security.*"

When our confidence is in the Lord we have nothing to fear; and only then, can one experience real security. "For the Lord shall be your confidence, firm and strong" (Prov. 3:26 AMP).

I Will Yet Praise Him

Why are you downcast, O my soul?
Why so disturbed within me?
Put your hope in God,
For I will *yet* praise him,
My savior and my God.

—Psalm 42:5 (NIV)

In the Swamp with Jesus[197]
by Jacquelyn Bradbard

Today is my Dad Jerry's birthday. He would be turning 70!
The loss has been intense this week. I took his picture in April
when we were facing the cancer battle and I encouraged him to
get outside for a walk. It was such a tough journey, yet I am so
thankful for him and that I could walk with him through it. And he
was truly courageous. But now he is gone and I have many
questions and fewer answers. It has been a more painful journey
than I can articulate yet. The grief process feels like I'm trudging
through a swamp. The waters are waist high and dark but I'm
determined to find my way through. Jesus reminded me one night
that I am not alone. He is in the swamp with me. Walking through it
by my side. Thankful for that! I miss you Dad. Happy 70th in
Heaven!! Love, Jacqui

Author's Postscript—Jerry and I became friends in college and were
blessed with many rich times of ministry and fellowship in the Lord.
Just prior to Jerry's home-going to glory in 2016, we spent a blessed time
with him and his wife reflecting on the grace, goodness, and faithfulness
of the Lord. I was deeply encouraged by Jerry's unflinching courage and
steadfastness of faith as he battled to win out over cancer.

No More Gloom

Nevertheless, there will be *no more gloom* for those who were in distress. In the past, he humbled the land of Zebulun and the land of Naphtali, but in the future, he will honor Galilee of the Gentiles, by the way of the sea, along the Jordan—

The people walking in darkness have seen a great light; on those living in the land of the shadow of death a light has dawned.

You have enlarged the nation and increased their joy; they rejoice before you as people rejoice at the harvest, as men rejoice when dividing the plunder.

For to us a child is born, to us a son is given and the government will be on his shoulders. And he will be called Wonderful Counsellor, Mighty God, Everlasting Father, and Prince of Peace.

—Isaiah 9:1—3, 6 (NIV)

"God, Heal That Baby!"[198]

by Dr. Dan Stephens

Each time God gives you a blessing, you have to build a little monument to it. Then, when you're surrounded by floods of despair and frustration, you can see those monuments standing above the flood waters and remember those blessings.

I'm a doctor at Karanda Mission Hospital in Zimbabwe. When I walk the wards of the hospital, I see about one-third of our patients suffering from AIDS.

Of those dying from AIDS, we have babies. We have 15 year-old girls, who were just beginning their lives. We have grandmothers 75 and 80 years old. We have 4 year-olds, and all ages in between. All of them are dying.

I struggle for months over a little baby, thinking perhaps it has AIDS, maybe malnutrition. I don't know. The child dies, and the test comes back. It's probably AIDS. The father has it and the mother has it—the infection at least.

Sometimes I'm called to the hospital three or four times in one day about a baby, who I know is going to die. I think, "Don't call me anymore ... the baby is going to die. It's bad enough having to see the baby ... just leave me alone" ... but they call me back down again.

On the way to the hospital, I say, "God if it's your will, you can heal that baby. I know you can. Just show me one time that you're going to heal that baby." The infant dies a few hours later, and I say, "Well, I knew it."

You really get discouraged if you think about what you would do if you were God. That's when you have to remember that God never asks you to understand Him. He asks you to trust Him.

"Trust in the Lord with all your heart and lean not on your own understanding; in all your ways acknowledge Him, and He will make your paths straight" (Prov. 3:5–6 NIV).

I've known these verses since I was a child. The message is so obvious, but I hardly ever think about it. God doesn't expect me to understand Him, and I shouldn't try to. I know this much: God does use the diagnosis of AIDS to bring many to Himself.

But mostly I just keep my eyes on those monuments standing above the floodwaters.

Prisoners of Hope

Return to your fortress, O prisoners of hope.
—Zechariah 9:12 (NIV)

Fortress of hope for earth's sore distressed. Grace upon entering
this sanctuary eternal. Impart your cherished balm—oh so
blessed. May mercy offset distress so vexing, so infernal.

Secure indeed this refuge amid a world a-crumbling,
Enabling prisoners who groan and stumble
To know a way beyond mere coping, Strengthened
in heart and, yes, now hoping.

Speak, majestic, perfect law of liberty. Let all who hear be
ransomed—free! Yes, bind all weary hearts to thee,
To gaze more fully upon yon budding tree of Calvary.

Now, break forth, oh, glorious dawn— Command all
unsettling shadows flee; Yes, shine ever more brightly and
free. Shed the light of life on all who embrace thee.
—CFG

"On the Waters of Sorrow"[199]

by Frances J. Roberts

"O my child, I am coming to you walking on the waters of the sorrows of your life; yes, above the sounds of the storm you shall hear MY voice call your name. You are never alone, for I am at your right hand. Never despair, for I am watching over and caring for you. Be not anxious.

"What seems to you to be at present a difficult situation is all part of MY planning, and I am working out the details of circumstances, so that I may bless you and reveal myself to you in a new way.

"As I have opened your eyes to see, so shall I open your ears to hear, and you shall come to know me *even as Moses did, yes, in a face to face relationship*. For I will remove the veil that separates ME from you, and you will know ME as your dearest Friend and as your truest Comforter.

"No darkness will hide the shining of MY face, for I shall be to you as a bright star in the night sky. Never let your faith waver. Reach out your hand, and you shall touch the hem of my garment."

> He caused the storm to be still,
> So that the waves of the sea were hushed.
>
> —Ps. 107:29 (NASB)

Defined or Refined?

It would not be too far from the truth to say that at the
end of the day, one's afflictions and trials of faith will
do one of two things, namely: define or refine us.
If we permit our trials *to define* us, we will then find
ourselves leaning toward a perspective on life that may well
become decidedly negative and filled with dismay.
However, if we permit trials of faith to *refine* us, we will
then by God's grace be poised to discover that our outlook
on life will be decidedly more hopeful and grace-filled.
—CFG

"The Faith Ante Rises"[200]

by Debbie Eichner

My health continues to be the driving force of my journey of faith. In recognition of my absolute need of Him, I kneel before the cross on a daily basis.

I have been fighting with bowel complications since birth. My condition increased in severity throughout childhood, owing to intractable constipation associated with IBS (Irritable Bowel Syndrome) and exacerbated by severe endometriosis. This disease resulted in 15 different surgical procedures and the eventual removal of my bowel (colon), including a full hysterectomy. Had it not been removed surgically, it would have slowly killed me.

Subsequently, my job security of 17 years, was lost owing to the economic downturn. Recently, God has upped the "ante of faith". Today I received a letter stating that I may not be able to work any longer, and if I do, I may lose ALL my disability benefits. The timing could not be worse, with my health deteriorating, and the bills going up.

So, on this very day I have been literally thrust to my knees and forced to lay out the very existence I live before God, reminding Him of His promises, namely: that His character is unchangeable and that because of this I know two things. He must fulfill His promises as laid out in template form I find in His Word; and secondly, I am confident that He can do all things for my good and His glory.

This major employment development, along with my present health status, will, by being in the realm of the sovereignty of God be one spectacular show of His power, yes, near unto the seas parting long ago and DRY LAND resulting for easy walking.

Should all rights be denied me, I have been told I will live on nothing, until my claim again goes through (in one-two years). But despite what dead-ends I see all around me right now, as I look back at God's faithfulness, both in the Bible and in my family's life and then my own, His character shows me His depth of love for His own. He wants us to look at Him, unflinchingly, to tell others of what is going on, always mindful to bring praise and honor to Him in the process, as you stand and watch the deliverance.

He does not want to only part waters that others say are impossible, He wants us to walk on dry land, sure-footed, for all to see who His own are, and to what lengths He will go to provide for them as they refuse to sit down, but stand into the wind and call out His words back to Him, tears pouring down our faces, knowing that in His time, He only can get the glory.

I think that my broken, battered body has been given to me as a gift and a responsibility: the gift is that through it I can share about Christ and glorify Him, as He is mightily lifted up through weakness. I claim no credit for anything that has been accomplished in and through this shell. The responsibility is that I am to manage this body to the best of my ability until I meet Jesus face-to-face. Then, I can release it and never have pain again! The two are very inter-connected. From my sick-bed, I have spent thousands of hours listening to others pour out their own pain and hurt; those who need comfort, encouragement, or a kick in the pants! Seriously, we have walking wounded all around us with nobody to listen. It takes a sick person to listen to needy people sometimes.

Having come this far, I know that God is at work showing Himself through the body He created with purposefulness and in His sovereign perfection. With it, I ask Him to show those in my life His faithfulness, as they watch not only the physical struggles, but how the large medical bills that match such a body, are met. And, wouldn't you know it? Just when I could not see how God would provide, He graciously strengthened me to work a further eight years. Yes, I stand in Him—knowing that in Him and through Him all things are possible and in this I can have and do possess peace and joy in abundance.

O Lord, be gracious to us; we long for you.
Be our strength every morning, our salvation *in time of distress.*
—Isaiah 33:2 (NIV)

Little Handful of Thorns[201]

Jeremy Taylor was a seventeenth-century English cleric, who was severely persecuted for his faith. However, even though he was imprisoned, his house was plundered, his family left destitute, and his property confiscated, he continued to count the blessings he could not lose. In 1645 he wrote:

> They have not taken away my merry countenance, my cheerful spirit, and a good conscience; they have still left me with the providence of God, and all His promises ... my hopes of heaven, and my charity to them, too, and still I sleep and digest, I eat and drink, I read and meditate. He that hath so many causes of joy, and so great, should never choose to sit down on his little handful of thorns.

Thou has put gladness in my heart, more than in
the time that their grain and wine increased.
—Ps. 4:7 (KJV)

Whirlwind Experiences[202]

by J. S. Holden

J.S. Holden cautions believers, who jest about the consequences of not heeding God's wake-up call, after intentionally playing with sin.

Holden said, "In as much as God loves that man, He sends the whirlwind upon his life, a whirlwind which…breaks up his false serenity and self-complacency.

The calamity in that man's life is not that God sends the whirlwind as God's chariot; (but) that he becomes hard…and nurses cold anger against God, because of what he regards as a cruel invasion of his rights."

May God in His mercy, prevent us from such impudent tone-deafness to the clarion call from His most gracious Spirit to our hearts.

Lesser Answers[203]

So often various biblical commentators and pastors have attempted to lead us to understand that the book of Job was composed, so that we might discover an answer for the perennially-nagging question of why the righteous suffer.

Greenslade observes that one of the lessons we may derive from reading the book of Job is to learn the importance of not accepting "*lesser answers*," until we find ourselves in the presence of the one who asks the more central questions, the answers to which often remain secure in the vault of God's heart.*

> My ears had heard of you but now my eyes have seen you.
> Therefore, I despise myself and repent in dust and ashes.
> —Job 42:5-6 (NIV)

---

* For further study, the reader may find the following theories useful in terms of understanding how various ones have sought to explain the reasons for Job's affliction of body and soul. In essence, each person (below) is suggesting that God is either being: Vindictive, retributive, furtive, instructive, or protective in his actions.

Vindictive – (Job's wife) – Job 2:9-10

Retributive - (Job's "friends" – Eliphaz, Bildad, Zophar, Elihu) – Job 4:8

Furtive - (Job) – 13:20-28; 23:1-9

Instructive - (Elihu)- Job 33:14-33

Protective - (God) - Job 38:2 ff. - God finally and effectively impresses on Job that he needs to trust God's heart, when he cannot perceive his hand (reasons for suffering). If you will, God did not want Job to come to the wrong conclusions, and conclude, "ah, so now I finally discover what God is really like!"

When the Mist Arises

by CFG

> The rising sun will come to us from heaven, to shine on
> those living in darkness and in the shadow of death, to guide
> our feet into the path of peace. —Lk. 1:78–79 (NIV)

On the occasion of sending congratulations to friends of ours, who were celebrating the arrival of their newest grandchild into a world beset with sadness and hardship, I related the following account, borrowed from a page in our journal.

I am reminded of a walk I had taken in the early 1980s at Udu Dam in Nyanga, a region located in the stunningly beautiful, eastern highlands of Zimbabwe. Having just enjoyed a cup of freshly brewed tea at the chalet and leaving Joyce and the girls to remain warm by the fireplace, I set out alone on my walk beyond the dam and over the nearby hillside on that rather crisp, but invigorating holiday morning.

As I ambled about on that bracingly cold morning, I noticed that mist was slowly lifting from the dam and adjacent landscape. Lifting my eyes further to survey what the morning mist had been covering on the hillsides, I was somewhat taken aback and speechless at first, as it occurred to me that the ground was burnt as far as I could see.

Walking further, it began to slowly dawn on me that there had been an extensive fire, which had swept up from the valley prior to our arrival at the chalet. However, I was not aware of the full extent of the fire, as it had not reached the immediate area surrounding the chalets.

It was then that I also saw a most unexpected, yet riveting sight that arrested my attention even more. In spite of the ravages from the devastating fire on all that lay in its path, and incredible as it seemed, new life had actually begun to emerge from the compacted soil all around me. Here and there I noticed small, delicate yellow flowers and tufts of green grass pushing up through the darkened landscape. This was a sight I was not soon to forget, nor ever want to.

As I continued on this invigorating journey, I came to realize how taken up I had actually become with this remarkable sight. It was then that the Lord began to stir within me the realization that these flowers portrayed for me irresistibly dramatic and yet poignant representations of God's incredible grace, which so vividly appear along the pathways of the harsh realities that burn their way through our life on occasion.

Understandably, this experience constituted for me both a dramatic and yet a symbolic analogy of what one may hope for when Jesus draws near to impart renewed grace and strength of heart to carry on, especially after a devastating experience portends to leave only ash and destruction in its harsh wake.

As a result of this unique experience, I often find myself looking out for flowers of grace, which the Lord Himself causes to spring up along the varied pathways we traverse in our lifetimes.

Surely then, it is fair to infer that with the coming of each new life and the prospect of hope it brings to our darkened world that we may take heart as we are reminded of yet another, yes, very special birth that did bring true living hope. Obviously, Jesus was no ordinary child. His coming brought hope to light through the cross and the empty tomb. With His glorious triumph over sin and death, He not only enables us to face the distresses of our temporal turmoil in the light of *His* gracious promises, but better yet, He causes the mist to arise, *as surely as it must and will continue to do, when the day spring from on high arises on our horizon by His glorious presence!*

It Never Occurred to Me[204]

It never occurred to me to question God's doings while I was an inmate of Auschwitz ... I believe my faith in God was not undermined in the least. *It never occurred* to me to associate the calamity we were experiencing with God, to blame Him ... or cease believing in Him at all.

—Reeve R. Brenner

Bibliographic Data

Much now seems clear to me in regard to the nature of God.
God's goodness is not something I get to decide upon.
I am a human being with limited understanding.
—J. B. Smith[205]

The Lord is good, a refuge in times of trouble. He cares
for those who trust in him... —Nahum 1:7

Augustine's Blessed Fault[206]

God judged it better to bring good out of evil,
Than to suffer no evil at all.
— Augustine of Hippo

You intended to harm me, but God intended it for good
to accomplish what is now being done,
the saving of many lives.
— Gen. 50:20 (NIV)

Endnotes, Attributions and Permissions

1   Charles Colson, *Answers to Your Kid's Questions* (Carol Stream: Tyndale House Publishers, © 2000. Used by permission of Tyndale House Publishers, Inc.), 31.

2   Ben Jonson, *Prose Quotations from Socrates to Macaulay* (Philadelphia: J.B. Lippincott and Co.), 1880.

3   C. S. Lewis, *A Grief Observed* (London: Faber and Faber, 1961. Used by permission of C. S. Lewis Pte. Ltd.), 5.

4   Wilfred Strom, permission granted by e-mail correspondence, 2016.

5   Wayne Grudem, *Systematic Theology* (Grand Rapids: Zondervan, 1994), 1147.

6   Taken from *Where is God When It Hurts?*, by Philip Yancey, Copyright © 1990, 1977, by Philip Yancey. Use by permission Zondervan, 261.

7   Deborah Colones, personal testimony. Used by permission of Mrs. Colones.

8   *The Dust Diaries,* by Owen Sheers, chronicles the pioneer missionary work of Arthur S. Cripps at Maronda Mashanu Mission in Southern Rhodesia. (London: Faber & Faber, 2004). Permission granted to cite excerpted material under terms of "fair use" by HMH Trade Publishing, NY.

9   C. S. Lewis, The Screwtape Letters (New York: Harper Collins, 2009).

10 Jeff Lucas, *Life Every Day Sep/Oct 2006, Elijah: Prophet at a Loss* (Surrey: CWR, 2006). Used by permission.

11 Charles H. Spurgeon, *Morning and Evening* (Ross-shire, UK: Christian Focus Publications, 1994), 556.

12 Watchman Nee, *The Normal Christian Life* (Fort Washington: CLC Publications, 1957 by Angus I. Kinnear). Used by Permission of CLC. May not be reproduced. All rights reserved.

13 Joanie Yoder, *Our Daily Bread* (Grand Rapids: Radio Bible Class), reprinted by permission. All rights reserved. © 2003 by RBC Ministries.

14 Evans, cited by Philip D. Yancey, adapted from *Where Is God When It Hurts?* (Grand Rapids: Zondervan, 1990, 1997). Published by permission of Zondervan.

15 Russell Kelfer, *Purpose Driven Life*, (Grand Rapids: Zondervan, 2002), 26.

16 Beth and Matt Redman, *Blessed Be Your Name* (2005, UK, Survivor Records, SURCD5026, CD 2005), permission granted to reprint, License #581551 Capitol CMG Publishing.

17 Ross McCordic (Dr.), used by permission of Mrs. D. McCordic (2016).

18 Ecclesiastes 11:8

19 Psalm 55:5-8

20 Attributed to Aeschylus, *The Oresteia*, 500 BC.

21 John Calvin, Tracts and Letters, Banner of Truth Trust, Edinburgh

22 A general perusal of the internet will reveal numerous renditions of these words of assurance.

23 John Piper, *Future Grace* (Sisters: Multnomah Publications, 1995). Used by permission.

24 C. S. Lewis, *A Year with C. S. Lewis—The Problem of Pain* (San Francisco: Harper Collins, 2003). Used by permission of C. S. Lewis Co. Poole, Dorset.

25 Content taken from *The Trivialization of God,* by Donald McCullough. Copyright © 1995. Used by permission of NavPress. All rights reserved. Represented by Tyndale House Publishers, Inc., 60.

26 Olevianus & Ursinus. *Heidelberg Catechism* (Albany: AGES Digital Library, 1563), 27.

27 John Eldredge, *The Journey of Desire* (Nashville: Thomas Nelson, 2000), 190.

28 John Maxwell, *A Leader's Heart* (Nashville: Thomas Nelson, 2010), 235.

29 James Montgomery, "The Vale of Tears," cited in *Bartlett's Familiar Quotations: The Issues of Life and Death*, 10th ed. (Boston: Little and Brown, 1919).

30 William James, *(ed. by V. Havner), Varieties of Religious Experiences: Circumspection of the Topic (In Tune with Heaven), Lecture No. 2* (Grand Rapids: Baker Books, 1990), 17. Used by permission.

31 19 words from CONFESSIONS by Saint Augustine, translated with an introduction by R.S. Pine-Coffin (Penguin Classics, 1961). Copyright © R. S. Pine-Coffin, 1961. Used by permission of Penguin Random House, U.K.

32 Charles Swindoll, *Great Days with the Great Lives* (Nashville: Thomas Nelson, 2005).

33 Luther, cited by William S. Plummer, *Psalms* (Edinburgh: Banner of Truth, 1975), 522. Public Domain.

34 Nathan and Scott Whitaker, citing William McNamara, *The One Year Impact for Living Men's Devotional* (Wheaton: Tyndale © 2016), May 1 reading. Used by permission under terms of fair use.

35 Isaac Watts, "Am I a Solder of the Cross?" 1724. Public Domain

36 Chip Ingram, *Life Lessons for Dry Seasons* (Dallas: Kindred Spirit, vol. 27, no. 2, 2003), 14. Used by permission, under terms of fair use.

37 Cyndi Olsen, used by permission—granted by e-mail correspondence (2016).

38 Charles H. Spurgeon, *Morning and Evening* (Ross-shire: Christian Focus Publications, UK, 1994), 472.

39 Phillip Greenslade, *Cover to Cover Every Day: Sept/Oct 2006, 2011,* "Representative Suffering" (Surrey: CWR, 2006, 2011). Used with permission.

40 Johann J. Schutz, *The Covenant Hymnal, Bohemian Brethren Kirchengesange,* "Mit Freuden Zart" (translated by: Frances E. Cox), (Chicago: Covenant Press, 1973), hymn no. 1.

41 C. S. Lewis, *A Grief Observed* (London: Faber and Faber, 1961), 5–7.

42. C.S. Lewis, "The Problem of Pain," In *A Year with C.S. Lewis* (San Francisco: Harper, 2003), 305.

43 George Herbert, *The Temple*, "The Bag" (1663).

44 Charles H. Spurgeon, *Treasury of David*, "Psalm 73" (Grand Rapids: Kregel Publications, 1968), 312.

45 John Koessler, cited in *Today in the Word*, "Theology Matters" (Chicago: Moody Bible Institute, May, 2004), used by author's permission.

46 Ira D. Sankey and Annie Herbert Barker (Arranger, 1883). Courtesy Cyber Hymnal, Hymnary.org, Calvin College, public domain.

47 Charles H. Spurgeon, *Treasury of David*, "Psalm 73:1" (Grand Rapids: Kregel Publications, 1968).

48 Isaiah 54:10 (NASB)

49 C. S. Lewis, *A Year with C. S. Lewis*, "The Great Divorce" (San Francisco: Harper Collins, 2004), 320. Used by permission.

50 Frank E. Graeff (1860–1919), *African American Heritage Hymnal*, #428, Hymnary.org (Calvin College).

51 Mariah Carey assures fans on her website. Further commentary available on various web-sites, hosted by CNN.com, PEOPLE.com, The Telegraph (UK), Enews, etc.

52 Victor E. Frankel, citing F. Nietzsche in: *Man's Search for Meaning* (Boston: Reprinted by permission of Beacon Press. Copyright ©1959, 1962, 1984, 1992).

53 Bernie May, writing on the significance of martyred missionary Chet Bitterman's life. Cited by Dr. Richard Winchell in TEAM Horizons, Wheaton, 1981.

54 Martin Ricquebourg. Used by permission of author.

55 Os Guinness, *The Call* (Nashville: Thomas Nelson, 2003), 59.

56 W.S. and C.D. Martin (1905), Trinity Hymnal, (134), Hymnary.org, public domain.

57 Primary sources accessed for research purposes: *Today in the Word* (Moody Bible Institute), and Kay Emmet, 'The kid in the bathtub': Twenty years later (The Bismarck Tribune, Feb. 12, 2012).

58 Charles H. Spurgeon, *Morning and Evening* (Ross-shire, UK, Christian Focus Publications, 1994), 568.

59 Charles Gaskill, personal testimony. Used by permission.

60 William Barclay, *The New Daily Study Bible*, "The Gospel of Matthew," vol. 1. Used by permission of Westminster John Knox Press. (London: John Knox Press, © 2001), 130.

61 David Gauthier, *Smyrna: Grace Under Fire*: SermonCentral.com (Internet sermon notes), 2000.

62 Taken from *Following Christ by* Joseph M. Stowell, Copyright © 1996, by Joseph M. Stowell. Use by permission of Zondervan, 202.

63 Eddie Cross, quote from his weekly news updates—used by permission.

64 Paul Van Gorder, *Our Daily Bread* (Grand Rapids: RBC, 1992), reprinted by permission. All rights reserved.

65 C. S. Lewis, *The Four Loves* (New York: Harcourt, Inc., 1988), 190.

66 Jonathan Edwards, cited in *Today in the Word* (Chicago: Moody Bible Institute, Oct. '99), 23. Reprinted by permission.

67 Feodor M. Dostoevsky, *The Brothers Karamazov,* translated by Garnet (New York: W.W. Norton, 1976), 216–17. Used by permission.

68 Taken from *Closer Walk by Bruce Wilkinson (citing* Johann Peter Lange), Copyright ©1992, by Bruce Wilkinson. Use by permission of Zondervan, 219.

69 Andrew Murray, *31 Days of Praise* (Day 17)—mforeman.com/laurie/.

70 Luis Palau, *Where Is God When Bad Things Happen?* (New York: Doubleday, 1999), 212.

71 The reader may wish to reflect on the wonderful words found in the hymn: *Great is Thy Faithfulness,* by T. Chisholm and Runyan

72 Elizabeth Osborn, *Never Alone* (Grand Rapids: The Tract League), verse 3.

73 Hugh Stowell, "From Every Stormy Wind that Blows," (1828). Hymnary.org. Public Domain

74 Carolina Sandell Berg, Text copyright © 1925 Board of Publication Lutheran Church in America admin. Augsburg Fortress, 382. Reproduced by permission.

75 James Reston, "World Morality Crisis," *New York Times* (July 6, 1968), license granted and used by permission.

76 The reader may enjoy: *How to Stay Sane,* by Philippa Perry, which is an insightful book on establishing a realistic balance in the turbulence of life. (London: Pan McMillan, 2012), 3.

77 Augustine of Hippo, *City of God,* trans. by H. Bettenson (London: Penguin, 1984), 14.

78 Rev. Joe Wright, Pastor Central Christian Church, Wichita. His prayer was offered in the Kansas State House, Snopes.com, E-Verify, Jan. 23, 1996—

79 Archibald Macleish, *J.B.* (Cambridge, Houghton-Mifflin Co., 1958), 11. Used by permission.

80 Steven Charnock, *The Existence and Attributes of God* (Minneapolis: Klock and Klock, 1977), 538.

81   Robert Louis Stevenson, *Songs of Travel and Other Verses*, "Song XXXI" (London: Chatto and Windus Publications, 1896, 49 (Public Domain) - Often cited under title: Poem for Sister Marianne Cope.

82   Gracia Burnham (with Dean Merrill), *To Fly Again: Surviving the Tailspins of Life* (Wheaton: Tyndale House, 2006).

83   Charles H. Spurgeon, *Treasury of David*, "Psalm 73" (Peabody: Hendrickson Publishers, 1988).

84   Tracy Beighly (ed.), *Today in the Word* (Chicago: Moody Bible Institute, 1999), 220.

85   Friedrich von Hugel, *The Mystical Element of Religion As Studied in St. Catherine of Genoa*, (London: J.M. Dent & Co., 1909), 264.

86   Charles H. Spurgeon, *Treasury of David* (Peabody: Hendrickson Publishers, 1988), 246.

87   70 words from CONCERNING THE CITY OF GOD by St. Augustine, translated by Henry Bettenson, introduction by John O'Meara (First published in Pelican Books 1972, reprinted in Penguin classics, 1984). Translation copyright by (c) Henry Bettenson, 1972. Introduction copyright (c) John O'Meara, 1984. Used by permission of Penguin Random House, U.K.

88   Luis Palau, (ibid.), 212.

89   Annie S. Hawks, *Great Hymns of the Faith* (Grand Rapids: Zondervan, 1980), hymn no. 318.

90   Bill Bright, *God: Discover His Character* (Orlando: New Life Publishers), 1999.

91   John Piper, *Future Grace* (Sisters: Multnomah Publications, 1995), 266–267.

92   John Bunyan, *Advice to Sufferers: The Works of John Bunyan*, vol. 2 (Edinburgh: Banner of Truth, 1991), 726.

93   William Shakespeare, *Hamlet*, Act III, Scene 1, Lines 63–64 (c. 1599–1602).

94   John Wesley, *Through the Year with Wesley* (London: Epworth Press, 1954), 9.

95   Charles Swindoll, *The Finishing Touch: Becoming God's Masterpiece* (Nashville: Thomas Nelson, 1994).

96   Charles H. Spurgeon, *Morning & Evening* (Ross-shire, Scotland, UK: Christian Focus, Publications, 1994), 472.

97   Horatio G. Spafford, *It Is Well with My Soul*, Faith Publishing House, 1873 (Public Domain).

98   Taken from *My Utmost for His Highest* (R) by Oswald Chambers (C) 1935 by Dodd Mead & Co., renewed (C) by the Oswald Chambers Publications Assn., Ltd. Used by permission of Discovery House, Grand Rapids MI 49501. All rights reserved, 135.

99   Warren Wiersbe, *Being a Child of God* (Nashville, Thomas Nelson, 1996), 201.

100 J.R.R. Tolkien's *The Lord of the Rings*, Two Towers, "The Stairs of Cirith Ungol," (New York: Ballantine Books, 1970, Special Ed.), 407. Used by permission (under terms of fair use) of HMH, Trade Publishing, USA.

101 Eugene Peterson, *A Long-Term Obedience in the Same Direction* (Downers Grove: IVP, 2000). Used by permission.

102 Charles H. Spurgeon, *Morning and Evening* (Grand Rapids: Zondervan, 1973), Feb. 12 (morning).

103 Robert Gee—permission to use this quote granted by e mail correspondence.

104 Genesis 31:42, (KJV).

105 Watchman Nee, *The Normal Christian Life* (Angus Kinnear, 1957), used by permission of CLC Publications. May not be further reproduced. All rights reserved.

106 Popularly attributed to an incident in the life of Rev. Charles H. Spurgeon.

107 William Cowper, *God Moves in a Mysterious Way*, 1774, Hymnary.org. Public Domain

108 Rick Warren, *The Purpose Driven Life* (Grand Rapids: Zondervan, 2002), 199.

109 Anonymous. Cited by Estela G-Adanza, IV Values Education, (Quezon City: Rex Book Store Publisher, 2006), 133.

110 John Eldredge, *The Journey of Desire* (Nashville: Thomas Nelson, 2000), 97.

111 27 words from PENSEES by Blaise Pascal, translated with a revised introduction by A. J. Krailsheimer (Penguin Classics 1966, Revised edition 1995). Copyright (c) A.J. Krailsheimer, 1966, 1995. Used by permission of Penguin Random House, U.K.

112 C.S. Lewis, *Perelandra* (New York: Scribner, 1944), 70.

113 Dietrich Bonhoeffer, *The Cost of Discipleship* (Nashville: B & H Publishing Group 1998). Used by permission, all rights reserved, 15.

114 Cassie Bernall, used by permission, Plough Publishing. The reader may find further commentary on Cassie's epic testimony, reported by Art Toalston, in the *The Layman,* (Nashville: Baptist Press, April 28, 1999).

115 C. S. Lewis, *A Grief Observed* (New York: Harper Collins Publishers, 1961), 65.

116 Caldwell's Union Harmony, *The Hymnal*, "How Firm a Foundation" (Waco: Word, 1986), 275.

117 Beth Moore, *Praying God's Word Day by Day* (Nashville: B & H, Cook Publications, 2006). Used by permission.

118 Charles Dickens, *Tale of Two Cities* (Philadelphia: Running Press Book Publishers, 1999), 11.

119 George Macdonald (cited by B. Barton and P. Comfort), *Life Application Bible*, (Wheaton: Tyndale House, 1993), 127.

120 Edward Hopper, *Great Hymns of the Faith*, "Jesus, Savior" (Grand Rapids: Zondervan, 1980), no. 303.

121 Warren Wiersbe, *Pause for Power* (Colorado Springs, Chariot Victor, 1995), 250. Used by permission.

122 William Bathurst (c. 1830), *Evangelical Lutheran Hymnary,* (Hymnary.org), public domain.

123 Ruth Bell Graham, *Decision Magazine* (November 2004), used by permission, BGEA.

124 Joseph Thon, *The Doctrine of Suffering*, doctoral dissertation defended in a public forum at the Roman Catholic Seminary of Brussels (recorded by hand by author, 1996).

125 The Hon. Ed Cross, *Linear History*, weekly personal e-mail correspondence, June 2005. Used by permission.

126 Eugene Peterson, *God's Message for Each Day*—January 31, "Five Smooth Stones for Pastoral Work " (Nashville: J. Countryman, 2004). Used by permission.

127 Millie Stamm, *Be Still and Know* (Grand Rapids: Zondervan, 1964), July 28 reading.

128 Taken from *Closer Walk*, by Bruce Wilkinson (citing A. Barnes), (c) 1992, by Bruce Wilkinson. Use by permission of Zondervan, 115.

129 Charles H. Spurgeon, *Treasury of David* (Peabody: Hendrickson Publishers, 1988).

130 Katharina von Schlegel, *Great Hymns of the Faith*, "Be Still My Soul" (Grand Rapids: Zondervan, 1980), 290.

131 William O. Cushing, *Great Hymns of the Faith* (Grand Rapids: Zondervan), hymn #282.

132 Alfred Lansing (citing Sir E. Shackleton), *Endurance* (Wheaton: Tyndale, 1999), ix.

133 Rick Warren, www.whatChristiansWanttoKnow.com.

134 Charles Swindoll, Excerpt from *The Origination of Something Glorious* "The Prophet of the Most-High" Copyright © 1991 by Charles R. Swindoll, Inc. All rights reserved worldwide. Used by permission. www.insight.org

135 The Quotable Lewis, *The World's Last Night and Other Essays* (New York: Harcourt, 1988), 4–5.

136 Martin Luther, cited in *Closer Walk* (Grand Rapids: Zondervan, 1992), 57.

137 C. S. Lewis, *The Problem of Pain* (Glasgow: William Collins and Sons, 1933), 24–25.

138 Haddon Robinson, used by permission of author via e-mail.

139 Luke 1:49 - The reader will enjoy reading Max Lucado's *Safe in the Shepherd's Arms* (Nashville: J Countryman, 2002), 30.

140 Charles Colson, *Answers to Your Kid's Questions*, "If God is Good, Why Is There Evil?" (Wheaton: Tyndale House, (c) 2000), 25–26. Used by permission of Tyndale House. All rights reserved.

141 Bodie and Brock Thoene, *All Rivers to The Sea* (Nashville: Thomas Nelson, 2000), 185–186. Used by permission of Thomas Nelson.

142 Wendell Phelps, cited in *Today in the Word* (Chicago: Moody Bible Institute, Oct. 1990), 10.

143 Harold Kushner, *When Bad Things Happen to Good People* (New York: Harper Collins, 1981), 42–44.

144 Hannah Whithall-Smith, *The Unselfishness of God* (New York: Fleming H. Revell, 1903), 219, public domain.

145 C. S. Lewis, *The Problem of Pain* (San Francisco: Harper Collins, 2003), 305. Used by permission.

146 James McGranahan (1891) and M. Cornelius, *Favorite Hymns of Praise* (496), Cyber Hymnal (Hymnary.org), public domain.

147 https://www.census.gov/people/disability, cited in Dallas Connection, (Dallas Seminary Press, 2010), Vol.10.

148 J.R.R. Tolkien, *The Lord of the Rings*, "The Two Towers," (New York: Ballantine Books, 1979, Special Ed.), 77. Used by permission (under terms of fair use) of HMH, Trade Publishing, USA.

149 Jonathan Edwards, "*The Pleasantness of Religion*," sermon (1723), public domain.

150 E.S. Lorenz (1876) and J.E. Rankin, Cyber Hymnal #6530, (Hymnary.org, Calvin College), public domain.

151 Malcolm Muggeridge), *A Twentieth Century Testimony*, (Nashville: Thomas Nelson, 1978).

152 Hugh Stowell (1828) and Thomas Hastings (public domain).

153 Sean Doyle (Rev.), extracted from his sermon on 1 Corinthians 10 (Harare: 2009), Used by permission of Rev. Doyle.

154 Ravi Zacharias, *Walking from East to West* (Grand Rapids: Zondervan, 2006), 12.

155 Taken from *Don't Waste Your Life* by John Piper, (c) 2003 by Desiring God Foundation, p. 61. Used by permission of Crossway, a publishing ministry of Good News Publishers, Wheaton, IL 60187. www.crossway.orgTaken from *Don't Waste Your Life* by John Piper, © 2003 by esiring God Foundation, pp. 61. Used by permission of Crossway, a publishingministry

156 George MacDonald, cited in *Today in the Word* (Chicago: Moody Bible Institute, 2002), 22.

157 John F. Walvoord and Roy B. Zuck. *The Bible Knowledge Commentary*, "2 Corinthians" (Wheaton: Victor Books, (c) 1985), 554. Used by permission of David C. Cook. All rights reserved.

158 Peter Kreeft, *Three Philosophies of Life* (San Francisco: Ignatius Press, 1989). 80. www.ignatius.com. Used with permission.

159 Gary Haugen, *By Faith*, "When the Will of God is Dangerous" (Lawrenceville: International Justice Mission, 2007), 15. Used by permission.

160 "Taken from Total Truth by Nancy Pearcy, (c) 2004, 26. Used by permission of Crossway, a publishing ministry of Good News Publishers, Wheaton, IL 60187, www.crossway.org."

161 Phillip Yancey, *Christianity Today* (Carol Stream: Christianity Today International, 1999), 104.

162 Phillip Yancey (citing Shakespeare), *Romeo and Juliet*, Act II Scene II, *Where Is God When It Hurts?* (Grand Rapids: Zondervan, 1990).

163 Katharina Von Schlegel, 1697–1797, public domain.

164 Warren W. Wiersbe, *Be Hopeful* (Colorado Springs: David C. Cook, 1982), 19–24. Copyright 1982 (c) Warren W. Wiersbe. Used by permission.

165 Taken from *My Utmost for His Highest* (R) by Oswald Chambers (C) 1935 by Dodd Mead & Co., renewed (C) by the Oswald Chambers Publications Assn., Ltd. Used by permission of Discovery House, Box 3566, Grand Rapids MI 49501. All rights reserved, August 10.

166 C. S. Lewis, *A Grief Observed* (London: Faber & Faber, 1961).

167 Pastor Ethan Moore, Excerpts from his pastoral care. Used by permission.

168 John E. Sanders, *The God Who Risks* (Downers Grove: IVP, 1998), 262. Used by Permission.

169 "Taken from *Roots of Endurance*, "Charles Simeon"by John Piper, (c) 2002, 77. Used by permission of Crossway, a publishing ministry of Good News Publishers, Wheaton, IL. 60187. www.crossway.org."

170 "Taken from *I Don't Have Enough Faith to Be an Atheist, by* N. Geisler and F. Turek, (c) 2004), 391. Used by permission of Crossway, a publishing ministry of Good News Publishers, Wheaton, IL. 60187. www.crossway.org."

171 Isaac Watts, *Works of Rev. Isaac Watts*, Book 3 (London: Longman, Hurst and Rees, 1813), Hymn 12, v. 6. Public domain.

172 Popularly attributed to Corrie Ten Boom. (Note to reader: there are several different versions of this poem in circulation, and for that reason many publishers find it difficult to verify the original source.)

173 John Donne, *The Works of John Donne*, "Devotions" Upon Emergent Occasions (London: J.W. Parker, 1839), 529

174 Diane Hawkins, used by notarized permission of Mrs. Hawkins.

175 Warren W. Wiersbe, *The Bumps Are What You Climb On*, "God Reigns" (Grand Rapids: Baker Books, 2002), used by permission.

176 John Piper, Desiring God: *Meditations of a Christian Hedonist* (Colorado Springs: Multnomah, 2011), 129–130. Used by permission.

177 Rev. Wm. H. Goold (ed.), *The Works of John Owen* (Edinburgh: Johnstone and Hunter, 1850), 284.

178 Harry Adams, *Kindred Spirit* vol. 29, no. 2. (Dallas: Dallas Seminary Press, 2005). Used by permission of Mrs. Susan Adams.

179 Pierre A. Renoir (in response to Matisse's query: "Why do you continue to paint, when you are in such agony?"), www.heismydelight.woodpress.com.

180 Keith Getty and Margaret Becker, "Jesus Draw Me Nearer," (Nashville: Thank You Music, 2002), license #581565 acquired from Capitol CMG Publishing and license #564815 acquired from Music Services.

181 George and Steven Sleigh (permission to use article granted by George Sleigh).

182 Isaac Watts (1719) and William Croft (1708), *Presbyterian Hymnal 210*, Hymnary.org. public domain.

183 Joe Stowell (ed.), *Today in the Word* (Chicago: Moody Bible Institute, October 1996), 22. Used by permission.

184 Dennis J. DeHaan, *Our Daily Bread*, ©2008 by Our Daily Bread Ministries, Grand Rapids, MI, reprinted by permission. All rights reserved.

185 The author is indebted to various background sources, but would like to express appreciation for a precis by Paula A. Kirk (ed.), *Closer Walk, A Woman with a Heart for God* (Grand Rapids: Zondervan, 1992), 52.

186 George MacDonald, *Our Daily Bread* vol. 49 (Grand Rapids: RBC Ministries, 2005).

187 Gerald Sittser, *Grace Disguised: How the Soul Grows Through Loss* (Grand Rapids: Zondervan, 1995), 154. Used by permission of Zondervan.

188 Alfred Edersheim, *Elisha the Prophet* (London: The Religious Tract Society, 1882), 156.

189 David Roper, *Our Daily Bread*, ©2016 by Our Daily Bread Ministries, Grand Rapids, MI, reprinted by permission. All rights reserved.

190 F.B. Meyer, *Closer Walk* (Grand Rapids: Zondervan, 1992), 344.

191 Joe Stowell (ed.), *Today in the Word* (Chicago: Moody Bible Institute, 1996), used by permission.

192 Excerpt(s) from *THIRTY-ONE DAYS OF PRAISE: ENJOYING GOD ANEW* by Ruth Myers with Warren Myers, copyright © 1994, 1996, 1997, 2003 by Ruth Myers and Warren Myers. Used by permission of WaterBrook Multnomah, an imprint of the Crown Publishing Group, a division of Penguin Random House LLC. All rights reserved.

193 William Cowper, *Psalms and Hymns—Divine Worship*, (Leicester: Wickes and Son, Printer, 1873), hymn #558, "Jehovah-Nisei." For further study, the reader may wish to refer to *The Poetical Works of William Cowper*, by Wm. Benham (ed.) 1874.

194 Hannah Whitall-Smith, *Perfect Peace* (Chicago: Moody Press, 2000), 86–87. Used by permission.

195 Phillip Schaff (ed.), *Homily 44 on the Gospel of John,* by John Chrysostom, bishop of Constantinople, series no. 1, vol. 14, (Buffalo: Christian Literature Publishing Co., 1889).

196 Millie Stamm, *Be Still and Know* (Grand Rapids: Zondervan, 1978), Nov. 17 Daily Reading. Used by permission. www.zondervan.com.

197 Jacquelyn Bradbard, a happy birthday tribute to her late father, Jerry Krellwitz, 2016. Used by permission.

198 Dan Stephens, *TEAM Horizons,* "God, Heal that Baby!" (Wheaton: TEAM Publications, July–August 1994). Used by permission of TEAM publications.

199 Frances J. Roberts, *Come Away My Beloved* (Urichsville: Barbour Publishing, Inc. 2002), 16. Used by permission.

200 Debbie Eichner, *The Faith Ante Rises*, personal testimony (used by notarized permission of Ms. D. Eichner).

201 Even though this material is regarded as being in the public domain (1645), the reader will find it, and many other encouraging testimonies of God's goodness to his people in: Robert J. Morgan: *Nelson's Complete Book of Stories, Illustrations, and Quotes.* (Nashville : Thomas Nelson Publishers, 2000), 737.

202 H. F. Stevenson (ed.), *Keswick's Triumphant Voice*, "God's Voice in the Whirlwind" (London: Marshall, Morgan & Scott, Ltd., 1963), 269.

203 The reader will appreciate the insightful biblical commentary and practical pastoral wisdom of Phillip Greenslade, inclusive of what some regard as his definitive work: The Big Story" (Surrey: CWR, 2010).

204 Reeve R. Brenner, *The Faith and Doubt of Holocaust Survivors* (London, UK: Transaction Publishers, 2014), 102. Used by permission.

205 Taken from *The Good and Beautiful God, by James Bryan Smith, Copyright (c) 2009 by James Bryan Smith. Used by permission of InterVarsity Press, P.O. Box 1400,* Downers Grove, IL 60515, USA. www.ivpress.com, 50

206 Augustine, "Felix Culpa" (Lt. Fortunate Fall), cited by Thomas Aquinas in *Summa Theologica* III (1, 3, ad 3).

207 Penelope Wilcock, *The Hawk and the Dove Trilogy* (Wheaton: Crossway Books, 2000). Used by permission under terms of fair use.

208 In public domain (Academy of American Poets). For further study: John Donne (Herbert Grierson, ed.), *Metaphysical Lyrics and Poems*, "Holy Sonnets" (Oxford, Clarendon Press, 1921).

So that no one would be unsettled by these trials.
You know quite well that we were destined for them.
—1 Thessalonians 3:3

Licenses and Royalties

Owing to the sheer volume of sources cited in this book, most of the permissions granted are on file with the author. However, where requested, "used by permission," is included in the End Notes, Attributions and Permissions segment of this book above.

Nevertheless, grateful appreciation is hereby expressed to all the publishers and individuals for permission to cite their copyrighted material or to refer to their work.

Special mention is also included for those companies that issued issued relevant licenses and to whom royalties have been paid.

License granted by Capitol CMG Publishing for *Jesus Draw Me EverNearer* by Keith Getty (words by M. Becker).

License granted by Capitol CMG Publishing for *Blessed Be Your Name* by Beth and Matt Redman.

The C. S. Lewis Company, Ltd., *The Problem of Pain*, by C.S. Lewis Copyright ©C.S. Lewis Pte. Ltd. 1940. *The Great Divorce* by C. S. Lewis copyright ©C.S. Lewis Pte. Ltd. 1946. The following extracts have also been reprinted by permission: *The Screwtape Letters*, *The Four Loves*, *The World's Last Night* and *A Grief Observed*. Royalties paid.

License granted by Music Services, Inc. for *Jesus Draw Me Ever Nearer -* Words by Margaret Becker.

New York Times, royalties paid to reprint "World Morality Crisis" by James Reston, © 1968.

Zondervan Corporation, Contract for Permissions include the following works:

The Purpose-Driven Life, by Rick Warren, Copyright (c) 2002 by Rick Warren; *Be Still and Know*, by Millie Stamm, Copyright (c) 1978 by Millie Stamm, and *Closer Walk*, by WALK THRU THE BIBLE MINISTRIES: Copyright (c) 1992.

Index of Authors Cited

About the Author

Chris Goppert was born and brought up in Southern California in a predominantly WASP culture. As a teenager, Chris assumed he was a Christian because he attended church.

However, when he heard about the grace and love of God for him as revealed in Jesus, Chris realized there was more to being a Christian than just attending church, and it was at that point he trusted Christ as his Savior at the age of nineteen, while attending university.

On the night of his conversion, Chris sensed the call of God upon his life to take the Gospel to others, whom he envisioned were waiting for someone to bring the Word to them, as it was brought to him through the faithful witness of a cousin.

After completing studies in college and an internship program, Chris and his wife, Joyce, went to what was then Rhodesia, Africa, (now Zimbabwe) in 1973 to commence missionary service with TEAM (The Evangelical Alliance Mission). In 1977, the Gopperts returned to America so Chris could complete his master's degree at seminary.

From 1978 to 2003, Chris and Joyce continued to serve full-time in Zimbabwe in various pastoral care, church establishment, and mentoring ministries.

After presenting with clinical depression and PTSD in 2003 (owing to their personal experiences of living through a liberation-struggle war, having observed protracted episodes of suffering and ministering in a pastoral care and nurturing context to those who suffered varying hardships), Chris and Joyce returned from Africa to America for a time of reflection and healing in a Christian restoration community. It was under the gracious and professional care of pastors and counsellors that Chris and Joyce were able to process in a structured way the emotional pain and grief they had absorbed during the course of their pastoral ministry to commercial farmers and their workers, who had been disenfranchised from their productive livelihoods and driven from their homes.

While spending some time away from ministry in Africa, the Lord directed Chris to begin writing *Drawing Strength from the Right Sources*. As a series of devotional and theological studies, Chris's book is designed to assist one to better comprehend some of the dynamics associated with personal suffering and hardships, to discern possible reasons why God may allow believers to suffer within the context of His will and what they can learn of God's essential goodness and integrity of heart through the process.

The Gopperts have two grown daughters whose husbands' employment has led them to serve in the beloved land of their birth and beyond.

Chris and Joyce are now retired from full-time ministry in Africa, having served in Zimbabwe under the auspices of TEAM (www. team.org) for over forty years, providing language acquisition skills for mission colleagues, members of the ex-pat community (NGOs), and friends in the community, whilst also teaching at a theological institution, speaking in local churches, and ministering in music and medicine, youth camps, and writing. Having many friends and family still in Zimbabwe, Chris and Joyce plan to return there each year to provide assistance in various ministry initiatives.

For all intents and purposes this book has no official ending, such as: "The End", or "and they lived happily ever after". The reason book has no ending, is because hard times do not end at a particular linear point in one's experience. Having said that, it is also encouraging to be reminded that there is also no end to God's faithful watch care and sustaining grace for all who look to Him, and trust to his mercy. Hence, the pertinence of Penelope Wilcock's most fitting words below.

> We can offer no simple solutions, no easy answers, to other people's tragedies. We can only be there. It is Jesus they need, not us, and even he offers no answers. He offers himself.
>
> —Penelope Wilcock[207]

"After you have suffered a while, the God of all grace, who called you to His eternal glory in Christ, will Himself perfect, confirm, strengthen and establish you"
— 1 Peter 5:10 (NASB)

That I May Rise and Stand!208

Batter my heart, three-person(*ed*) God
For you as yet,
But knock, breathe, shine and
Seek to mend.
That I may rise and stand
O'er throw me, and bend your force
To break, blow, burn and make me new.

—John Donne